"Funny, enigmatic and heartfe
emergency service. If you're stopped by the roadside of life, the wheels close to coming off, this book is a must."

Jamie McCall, VP Brand Marketing, Nike Direct EMEA

"Thank Christ for Gavin Oattes. To all the dreamers out there, get this book, start the dream today, not Monday, today. Put the phones down, get into cardboard boxes 'n' play cars, get outside with the kids and build a rope swing on a tree branch.

Enter a beard competition for no reason, be aware of the dickheads, but don't let the dickheads turn you into a dickhead, even if they won't let you go home when the arse of your trousers has ripped during work.

Post an orange to someone, find the Pirahã tribe, or find your tribe, stick with them, surround yourself with support.

Visit and love your parents before they head to the moon.

But most importantly...BE THE MILK!!!!

These are just some of the moments, and memories Gavin shares with his readers, I literally didn't put this book down, I nearly read it in one day!!! And that's saying something, as I'm thick as shit.

Buy it, love it, remember it."

Jason Byrne, Comedian and Radio Host

Life Will See You Now

Quit Waiting for the Light at the End of the Tunnel and Light That F*cker Up for Yourself

Gavin Oattes

CAPSTONE
A Wiley Brand

This edition first published 2020

Registered office
John Wiley & Sons Ltd, The Atrium, Southern Gate, Chichester, West Sussex, PO19 8SQ, United Kingdom

For details of our global editorial offices, for customer services and for information about how to apply for permission to reuse the copyright material in this book please see our website at www.wiley.com.

Library of Congress Cataloging-in-Publication Data
Names: Oattes, Gavin, author.
Title: Life will see you now : quit waiting for the light at the end of the tunnel and light that f*cker up for yourself / Gavin Oattes.
Description: Chichester, West Sussex, United Kingdom ; John Wiley & Sons, [2020] | Includes index.
Identifiers: LCCN 2019053598 (print) | LCCN 2019053599 (ebook) | ISBN 9780857088086 (paperback) | ISBN 9780857088130 (adobe pdf) | ISBN 9780857088147 (epub)
Subjects: LCSH: Self-realization. | Conduct of life.
Classification: LCC BJ1470 .O28 2020 (print) | LCC BJ1470 (ebook) | DDC 158.1—dc23
LC record available at https://lccn.loc.gov/2019053598
LC ebook record available at https://lccn.loc.gov/2019053599

A catalogue record for this book is available from the British Library.

ISBN 978–0–857–08808–6 (paperback) ISBN 978–0–857–08813–0 (ePDF)
ISBN 978–0–857–08814–7 (ePub)

10 9 8 7 6 5 4 3 2 1

Cover design and image: Peter Cotter

Set in Adobe Caslon Pro 10/14 by Aptara Inc., New Delhi, India
Printed in Great Britain by Bell and Bain Ltd, Glasgow

For those of us trying to find our place in the world, anyone who has ever felt different or just simply forgotten who they really are. And for those currently floating in a most peculiar way.

Contents

The Bit Before the Actual Start

A smidge of context. Me, I'm a 'Doctor of Happiness', so I made a pledge a few years ago that all my social media would be uplifting and positive. My Twitter account is followed by 10,000 primary schools, so I'm mindful of the audience. It's a big fat 'no' to ranting, grumbling and swearing and an equally obese 'yes' to happiness, kindness and unconditional love.

Gav, on the other hand. He's in the same marketplace as me but he doesn't seem to care who's tuning in. He's more edgy. A bit random. Often uplifting and sometimes a smidge sweary.

Now here's the thing. If you met me in actual real life you'd see that I'm a normal bloke from Derby with all the accumulated ranting, grumbling and swearing that comes with the territory. But if you met me on Twitter, FB or Instagram, I'm all nicey-nicey. I'm curated. Holding myself back. The social media me *isn't* the real me.

Whereas Gav's always unashamedly Gav. I doff my cap to that. Authenticity is built into Gav's DNA.

To butcher a long story to the bare bones, after bumping into each other at a conference Gav and myself eventually teamed up to write a book. We discovered that if you chuck a bit of his energetic bonkersness in with my science, it works a treat. We pioneered a 'laugh 'n' learn' approach in the common belief that, first and foremost, a decent personal development book has to be a rollicking good read. If you can *accidentally* learn a whole load of stuff along the way, then BOOM, that's a stand-out book in the genre.

We pioneered a new genre of 'self-help comedy'. Our first book *Shine* is worth buying just for chapter 3. I'd go so far as to say it's the best personal development chapter ever written and, guess what, it was written by Gav.

Shine shone so we did one for little people – *Diary of a Brilliant Kid* – which was like *Shine* but with no naughty words. We aimed it at kids aged 6 to 106 and that was fab too. It's worth buying for Gav's chapter about oranges.

Zest completed the trilogy and, once again, Gav's chapters stole the show. I was beginning to detect a pattern!

Fast forward to right now. My Gav trilogy complete, I took a breather while the canny Scotsman conjured this little rascal, his first solo project. And I promise you, it's an absolute belter.

Life Will See You Now raises the bar from 'laugh 'n' learn' to 'laugh, learn 'n' cry'. This book is very up close and personal, scoring a whopping 9.3 on the blub-factor (anything above 8 is *'have a tissue up your sleeve just in case'* and above 9 is *'almost certain to induce gentle weeping'*).

Because, here's the thing, our blue-blooded, ginger-bearded, fast-talking, keynote-speaking fearless Braveheart of a Scotsman is actually wracked with self-doubt. He makes mistakes. He's his own worst critic. He's riddled with insecurities.

And yet he's learned to plough on regardless.

Gav's petrified that you won't like this book.

But I'm confident you absolutely will. Gav's imperfections make him perfect. So, basically, he's just like you and me. If you give these pages a chance you'll learn to give up the struggle for perfection. It's a very refreshing message. Chill. You can quit the chase.

If you want to avoid the plot spoiler, look away now...

You don't have to strive to be the best in the world. Your job is to refocus on being the best FOR the world. That one word changes everything.

So find yourself a comfy place, switch off the distractions, open your mind (and your heart) and treat yourself to some 'self-help comedy'. Remember, just because it's funny doesn't mean it's not deadly serious.

Bon voyage!

Dr Andy Cope

Keynote speaker, bestselling author
and learning junkie

www.artofbrilliance.co.uk

CHAPTER 1

Basket Case

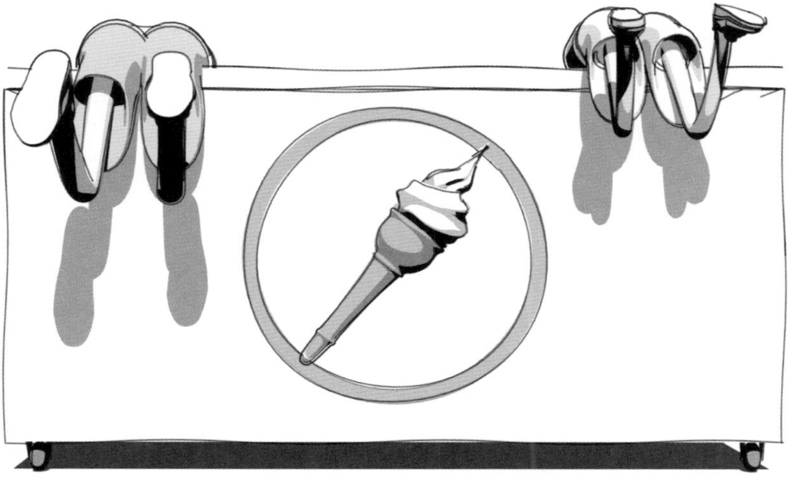

'I've yet to find a level of enthusiasm that tops "Holy shit look at this giant potato chip!"'

—Macaulay Culkin

It's so true isn't it? Doesn't matter who you are, where you're from, how cool you are or even what age you are, if you pull a massive crisp out of the bag you are *absolutely* going to turn to every other person in the room and share the outstanding news that you have pulled a gigantic piece of fried potato from a bag.

Ever since I was a wee boy, an abnormally large crisp has blown my mind. Even if I'm on my own I sit up and look around for someone to show! The great thing about modern days is the fact you can take a photo of it and instantly send it to everyone you know, and if you're particularly chuffed with your findings then you can of course share it with the entire human race on social media.

I also expect nothing less from you, dear reader. I know we're only 175 words in but from this moment on, each and every time you pull a share-worthy potato chip from the bag, I expect you to share it with me immediately! (@gavinoattes #MassiveCrisp)

I really wanted to start this book with a quote that would inspire you. A quote that would resonate, challenge and, perhaps most importantly, set the tone for what lies ahead.

I love an inspirational quote; they get me thinking. I do, however, prefer them if they're a little edgy, funny or quirky.

I searched long and hard, went through all my favourites and eventually whittled it down to my top three. I sat and stared at them for many minutes, agonizing over the choice that lay ahead. It wasn't happening.

So I decided to have a break, popped myself onto Twitter, and BOOM. There it was. The moment I had been waiting for, unexpectedly produced from the mind of a child superstar. Well, he's no longer a child but when you think of Macaulay Culkin there really is only one image that springs to mind.

Yup, Kevin. Kevin McAllister to be exact. The cute, cheeky and street savvy 8-year-old that lit up our lives with booby traps, mischief and a lovely cheese pizza just for him. Apparently – according to his cousin – he's 'what the French call les incompetents'.

Now, whether you were a fan of the *Home Alone* franchise or not, it's fair to say Kevin was anything but incompetent. He took us all on a journey, an exciting adventure that ultimately reminded us of the importance of love, bravery, family and making the most of what we have. Oh, and not relying on technology, particularly to wake us up before a flight!

I had no plans to start this book with a Macaulay Culkin quote but, ultimately, his words reflect what this book is all about. Seeing the beauty and wonder in everything. Even the ordinary, the everyday. Even a giant potato chip. It's about simplicity and appreciating all that's around us. Allowing ourselves to be excited at life, what it throws us, everything. It's about grit, zest and passion. It's about rediscovering that childlike wonder, living in the moment, getting through all sorts of shit and yes, having fun, lots of it, always.

It's about blowing your own goddamn mind for a change.

Because we're all going to die, right? But before we even begin to think about curtains of the final variety, does one not want to make sure the journey to the cloth shop is truly spectacular?

'Darling, one day you will die…so live to please the mind: keep good thoughts, look at the stars, and enjoy beautiful days.'

—J.S.

We're born, we live and then we die. Now only two of these are really guaranteed. If you're reading this now, then you've definitely been born, which in itself is extraordinary. And guess what? You're *definitely* going to die, which depending on *how* you go can also be extraordinary. The bit in between, however, is the part in question. This is the bit I want to focus on in this book: the middle.

Being born is mind blowing, but it's easy. Not for Mum, obviously, she does all the work, you did absolutely fuck all. Like dying, it just happens. Neither are particularly pleasant or enjoyable for anyone but for the individual on their way in or out, it's a piece of piss.

But do you believe in life after delivery?

Let's be blunt, life can be fucking shit. It requires energy and effort. It can feel like a chore but the more skilled at it we become, the better at it we get and the happier we feel.

We all have different thoughts and opinions when it comes to living our best life and what that even means. That's what keeps the world exciting, we're all different. But really, who has actually nailed living? Has anyone truly perfected life?

Nope, of course not. But we can give it a go!

Think back to when you were a wee kid and you saw your teacher *outside* of school, perhaps in the supermarket or in a restaurant. Remember how it made you feel? It was always one of life's real 'Holy fuck' moments. It was exciting, mind blowing, weird and incredibly warming all at once. And it kinda made us feel on edge a little.

This is how life should make us feel every day. Why? Because it *is* exciting, mind blowing, weird and incredibly warming.

And guess what? It kinda makes us feel on edge a little. This is what truly being alive *should* feel like.

Do you wake up every day buzzing? Now, depending on where you're from, the word 'buzzing' has many different meanings but you know what I mean. Pumped! Actually this word isn't any better…

Raring to go. That's better!

Are you happy most of the time? I'm going with 'most of the time' as we simply cannot be happy *all* the time.

Is there a great big enormous fire for life in your belly? Or have the flames that once burned bright been smothered by the blanket of broken dreams? Or perhaps gone out entirely?

What's the point in even having a belly if there's no fire in it, right?

Think back to you when you were about 4 years old. The fire was stoked daily. Just getting out of bed was exciting. I mean, for fuck's sake, watching mum and dad pee was exciting, *everything* was exciting! (Note: If you're still watching people pee, stop it, it's different when you're an adult.)

As a professional speaker, I often speak about the daily excitement I witness from my own children. Let me introduce them to you.

I have two kids and they'll both pop up throughout this book as we go along. My son is called Kian – it's an Irish name, meaning 'king'. For any pop music fans out there he wasn't named after the dude from Westlife. I wanted to call him 'Optimus Prime' but I wasn't allowed. I remember going to register his birth and being asked to write his name down. My hand paused over the paper for a moment…Optimus Oattes has ring to it. I totally shat it; my wife would never have forgiven me. Then the woman behind the desk asked the now infamous question…

'Does he have a middle name?'

Ooooh. Emmm. Geee.

I can write whatever I want.

I could hear the clock ticking.

C'mon Gav, answer the lady!

'Yes he does, he does have a middle name…'

Kian 'Optimus Freddie Mercury The Second, He-Man Gallus Prime' Oattes.

I'll let you decide if that's true or not and for the non-Scottish readers out there I'll let you Google the word 'Gallus'.

I also have a daughter, Megatron Oattes. Not really, but that would have been sensational. Her name is Ellis and I'm going to tell you a little story about her and her big brother Optimus.

The most excitement I've ever seen in life, in another human (in this case two humans) in any one moment was in my children whilst on holiday in Menorca, 2015.

This was the first time we had ever been 'All Inclusive'. Everything included. EVERYTHING.

On day one it was 32 degrees and the kids asked if they could each have an ice lolly or an ice cream.

'Of course you can,' I said. I pointed to a giant freezer over beside the bar – the ones that require you to slide the glass open on the top – and told the kids they can go and help themselves.

'Can you give us the money?' asked Kian.

'You don't need any money, just go and help yourself,' I replied.

Ellis piped up, 'You can't just help yourself, Daddy, that's stealing.'

I explained the 'All Inclusive' concept again for the umpteenth time.

'So, we can just go and choose any one we want and we don't need to pay for it?' asked Kian.

'Correct.'

'*Any* ice cream, Daddy?'

'Yes, *any* ice cream.'

They both looked over at Mummy, who nodded and backed me up with 'That's right guys, what're you waiting for?!'

Now, this is where the moment happened. Both of them, with every ounce of their wee bodies began to wiggle with excitement, their wee faces lit up, smiles beaming from ear to ear. They pirouetted and off they went like two cartoon characters animated to perfection. Their wee wiggles made up of a sort of dance, run, hop, skip and a jump leaving a trail of smiles around the pool.

Now picture two tiny kids leaning into a giant freezer, both of them with both feet off the ground. This was their 'giant potato chip moment'. Happiness personified.

Pure. Fucking. Magic.

And throughout this book I want to help you find yours. It might just be something simple or it might be something huge. This book is your freezer, your bag of potato chips. Lean in, both feet off the ground, grab on with two hands and pull from it something that sets your fucking soul on fire.

I obviously hope you love reading it. I hope it makes you smile, laugh, think and, most importantly, feel something. If it doesn't then that's OK, I learned to accept a long time ago that I'm not everyone's cup of tea. You'll have realized by now that I'm a bit sweary, but the way I see it is that while I say bad words, I don't say bad things.

The way I see it is that through this book I have been given the opportunity to help people feel happier, more excited for life, thoughtful, inspired. I believe the world needs more of that.

So let's open up the crisps and dive into the freezer...

'You're a ghost driving a meat covered skeleton made from stardust, what do you have to be scared of?'

—Anon

39 Minutes and 38 Seconds

I woke as a 15-year-old for the first time. I could think of nothing cooler than having my birthday on a Saturday. Well, there was one thing cooler and that was having your 15th birthday on a Saturday *and* getting a brand new Sony Walkman. I also received a gift voucher for HMV. I threw on some clothes and headed for the train station, headphones round my neck, Walkman tucked in my pocket.

Half an hour later, with no idea what I was going to buy, I walked into HMV and I was drawn straight to one particular album. I can vividly remember the moment I picked it up in my hand, it was meant to be. I made my purchase and left the shop.

I had bought an album I'd never heard of by a band I'd never heard of. I liked their name, Green Day, it sounded weird. I liked the album title more, *Dookie*. Interesting word, Google it…

Upon exiting HMV I made the decision to make my way home by bus, something I had never done. The bus takes 55 minutes; the train takes 15. It's a no-brainer: train wins hands down. However, for whatever reason, the bus was to be my birthday carriage home. I got on the bus and with no one else to be seen, I sat down. I slowly tore the cellophane wrapper from my new purchase, popped the album into my Walkman, put my headphones on, and pressed play.

That was it.

For the next 39 minutes and 38 seconds I was transported to a place I'd never been before and from the opening riff my life changed forever. Fifteen-years-young and ready to take on the world. That sound, those lyrics. The hairs on the back of my neck stood up, I felt an inexplicable rush of adrenaline, and in just under 40 minutes I could see and feel all my dreams coming true. All my worries just seemed to vanish. The weight of the world that I wore around my neck gone. Never before had I felt so motivated in life, so energized, mobilized. Alive.

Happy. Truly happy.

I believe everyone has *that* album. The one that changed their life, and if it's not an album, then it's a film or a book or a show or maybe even a person.

One that brings hope, energy and big ideas into their lives. One that ignites that giant fire in our bellies. One that makes us feel invincible.

That album didn't just open my mind up to a particular genre of music, it opened my mind up to believing that dreams can come true.

The power of music. The power of lyrics.

The opening track for *Dookie* is an anthem for the apathetic and uninterested outcasts. Its lyrics are a direct ode to indifference. What I heard was a young wannabe wanting to stay young and immature forever, someone who doesn't want to face the reality of growing up. The difference between him and me though is that he was prepared to drown in all the pressures that come with adulthood and accept the inevitable passing of time. I wasn't. I'm still not. I am nearly 40 and do everything I can to stay young and immature. The world tells us to grow up. I consciously try my best to *not* feel like I'm growing up. Some would argue I am, in fact, growing down!

Then came track 2, 'Having a Blast'. I heard this song very much as a metaphor for bottled up emotions and anxiety. Don't worry, this is not just a track by track run down of an album but this track, along with track 5, 'Basket Case' really spoke to me. Again, all about anxiety. At 15 years of age I was the world's biggest worrier.

If I was a 1990s wrestler I'd be the Ultimate Worrier.

I worried about planes crashing, cancer, girls, rejection, boys, death, girls, bullies, weight, girls again and, well, more death. I worried myself sick, literally. I've never written about this before and I've told few people about my anxiety as a teenager.

It's important that I share this with you before we go any further as I want you to know who I am and what it means to me to be able to write what I'm writing. I've spent much of my life as simply a scared wee boy from Scotland. And guess what? I still am. I'm still that wee boy at heart but from that day, aged 15, I changed my mind about life. Well, to be more accurate I changed my mindset towards life.

That album put me on a new path.

I was a dreamer. Always had been. I had often heard the phrase 'Get your head out the clouds and stop dreaming, Gavin'. I made a real effort to focus in school, to really hear what was being said and taught. Sometimes I was successful and other times not so much. My ability to concentrate wasn't great. I still find it hard.

Many of us spend far too long contemplating life and all that goes along with it; thoughts, feelings or problems. Sometimes we just need to trust our gut instinct and go for it. I had a moment that day. It was time to get my head back in the clouds and start dreaming again.

'I would rather be ashes than dust!

I would rather that my spark should burn out in a brilliant blaze than it should be stifled by dry-rot. I would rather be a superb meteor, every atom of me in magnificent glow, than a sleepy and permanent planet. The function of man is to live, not to exist.

I shall not waste my days trying to prolong them.

I shall use my time.'

—Jack London

But before we go forward, for context, I need to take you backwards…

Fee-fi-fo-fum

So there I was, week 1 of primary school. Five years old and learning to fit in, whatever that fucking means.

It was Friday, the final day of week 1. My school experience so far had been outstanding. New friends, old friends, Hide-and-Seek and as much 'Heads Down Thumbs Up' as I could possibly imagine.

Magic.

We came back into the class after playtime fresh from a game of 'tig'. The head teacher, Miss Smart (real name) popped in for a chat.

'Good Morning boys and girls.'

'Gooooood Mmmmoooorrnning Miiiisss Smaart.'

Miss Smart was about to tell us something that would be a game changer for me.

'Boys and girls, for the first time ever, this Christmas, we are going to put on a school pantomime.'

I couldn't believe what I was hearing. A pantomime, in my new school. I loved pantomime.

'Not only are we putting on a pantomime, boys and girls, but we need some of *you* to be in it.'

Well, this just about sent me over the edge. *My* school was putting on a pantomime and some of *us* were going to be in it! I couldn't wait to tell my mum and dad.

'The Pantomime we will be doing this year is "Jack and The Beanstalk".'

My absolute favourite pantomime ever. I could see it in my mind. The giant's enormous mechanical legs walking across the stage as 'Fee Fi Fo Fum' rings out across the theatre.

'We need five pupils from this class to be the mice who run on stage every night and steal the giant's cheese.'

Mind. Blown.

I was imagining myself sitting in the audience with snacks a-plenty. I could see the mice, the cheese, and again, the giant's legs. And me. I could picture it. It was going to be hilarious.

I was experiencing an excitement I had never felt before. A rush of pure adrenaline that felt magic. It was new to me, and I liked it. I liked it a lot.

Throughout life we are presented with opportunities. I was about to be presented with one that would ultimately shape my entire life. I shit you not, what happens next changed everything for me.

Remember, I was five.

'Hands up if you want to be one of the mice in the pantomime?'

My hand was up the second she even began to say the word 'hands'. Imagine the fastest hand in the world. My hand was faster than this. Look at your own hand right now (I dare you). Go on, look at it and move it up into the air as fast as you can. So, the speed at which you just moved is amateur compared to the speed I moved my entire arm this day as a 5-year-old. Try again…still too slow. I was Bruce Lee fast. In fact, I was Bruce Lee.

'Gavin Oattes.'

She picked me! This was it; this was my moment.

'Your hand was up first; do you want to be a mouse?'

All of a sudden I could picture the audience from the stage. It was like the camera in my head spun around 180 degrees. Now there were hundreds of people sitting watching me. What if it went wrong? What if they didn't enjoy it? What if I wasn't good enough? What if no one turned up?

Where were all these questions coming from?

My wonderful feeling of unbelievable excitement turned to a much less-wonderful feeling of unbelievable fear. I was scared but this was not a scared I had ever felt before. This was new and I didn't like it.

My heart started to pound. I could hear the blood passing through my ears, my chest felt like it was crunching gears and my heart was racing faster than ever before. Shaking, nausea, numbness and, of course, impending doom.

I was five. I just wanted to be a mouse, I really did. More than anything in the world, but something, something deep inside was stopping me.

It felt like I was going to shit myself. This was a horrendous feeling of what I now know to be anxiety and what I came to discover as 'giving way too much of a fuck about what people think about me'.

Now at this moment it's important for me to be clear on something…

There are moments in life you should absolutely give a fuck. You really should, but only about things that set your soul on fire. As a human you need to save your fucks for magical shit.

'Do you want to be a mouse?' Miss Smart repeated.

Again, all I could see was the audience staring back at me. All of a sudden I knew what it meant to be a worrier.

'No thanks, I only put my hand up because I need to go to the toilet.'

Everyone laughed. I can distinctly remember thinking 'Something's wrong, something's wrong, something's wrong' over and over again.

My teacher stepped in…

'Are you sure Gavin? You seemed awfully excited.'

I had to get out. I repeated myself.

'I only put my hand up because I need to go to the toilet.'

'OK then, off you go,' she said as I ran out the door.

I ran all the way to the toilet, ran into a cubicle, locked the door and burst into tears. I had never felt like this before. Five years old and I felt like my world had come to an end.

Why was I feeling like this over a fucking pantomime?

Might seem a little over dramatic but to put this into a 5-year-old's perspective, it was my absolute dream to be in a pantomime. I had always wanted to be in one. This was my magical shit. I had my chance and I blew it.

Because I was scared.

Seven years of primary school passed and not once did I set foot on a stage through choice. Not once did I volunteer for anything that involved possible public humiliation.

That moment has stuck with me forever. I allowed the fear to get the better of me. That day affected my confidence for a very long time. It kinda still does.

Then came high school. Even with all the fears and all my anxieties, my dream was still to be on stage. I continued to turn down every chance I had to get up and perform; I was so worried about what others might think. I didn't pick drama and no matter how much I wanted to, I didn't audition for school shows. More opportunities passed. Even reading aloud from a book in class became an issue for me. My face would turn bright red and my classmates would laugh.

'Oattesie's taking a beamer,' they would say. I can't explain how much that knocks a 13-year-old's confidence, even if done in jest.

I was still dreaming of being on stage, performing and entertaining for hundreds (maybe thousands one day) of people in a theatre. By 15 years of age I was obsessed with comedy. Stand-up comedy, comedy films, TV shows, books, basically anything that was really silly and made me laugh. I would sit in my room at night writing comedy sketches, filling notebook after notebook with all the nonsense stored in my brain.

Maybe one day I would get to share this nonsense with the world.

People are a bit like belly buttons. Some of us are introverts (innies), some of us are extroverts (outies) and some are somewhere in the middle (inbetweenies).

It doesn't matter who you are, where you're from or what anyone else thinks of you. You are allowed to believe in you. You are allowed to be confident in you. You are allowed to step out of your comfort zone and when you spot an opportunity that looks and feels right, grab on with two hands, keep your feet on the ground and run as fast as you fucking can.

If you don't, then one day you might just look back and wonder, 'What if?'

At 18 years of age I finally went for it. If there was ever a job for someone terrified of crowds, public humiliation and other people's opinions, it certainly wasn't stand-up comedy.

So, naturally I became a stand-up comedian…

I did my first gig. It felt incredible. Over the last 20 years I have performed all over the world. Good gigs, terrible gigs, great gigs. So many ups and downs. I've met the most wonderful people and the main thing I have learned is this. If you're faced with an opportunity that's both terrifying and amazing, then you should totally go for it.

We're travelling at the speed of life. We need to stop the navel-gazing and go make things happen.

Earlier I wrote that children need to stop being told to get their head out the clouds and instead be encouraged to get their heads *back* in the clouds. Guess what? *Adults* need to get their heads back in the clouds, I need to get my head back in the clouds and the chances are you need to get your head back in the clouds, too. And start dreaming again. Like, proper dreaming, not sleep dreams. Actual big fuck-off dreams that excite you and get your heart racing. The kind of shit that gets you out of bed with an extra spring in your step.

The problem most of us have in achieving our dreams is our thinking. Our thinking helps us to quit, to not try. We've all felt it.

But it's our thinking, and only our thinking that will help us to succeed.

In the words of T.D. Jakes:

> 'It's an urge. If truth be told, every president has felt it, ever champion has felt it. Every king has felt it, every lion has felt it. Every winner has felt it, every soldier has felt it. Every victorious person has felt it...the urge to quit.
>
> Don't you give up on your dream. I don't care if you don't have the money, you don't have the help and you don't have the family for it, and you don't have the background for it, and you don't have the friends for it, don't you give up on your dream, don't you do it. Don't you do it, don't you do it.
>
> It may take you twice as long, you may have to take courses and classes, you may not read as fast, you might not move as quick, you

might not have as much, but don't you quit. Don't you quit. Don't you quit. You do make a difference. You do make a difference. You do make a difference.

As weak as you are. As tired as you are. As many mistakes as you made, you do make a difference. There is something they would lose if you were not there. There is something they would miss if you were not there, you do make a difference. You do make a difference. You do make a difference.'

This book is for people doing the best they can with what they've got. It's for those who feel they've hit rock bottom, and it's for those who just need a wee lift.

We live most of our life inside our head, we need to make sure it's a nice place to be.

Although it won't be everyone's cup of tea, this book is for everyone.

Life...we may not break any ribbons, we may not get any trophies, but if we can learn to hang on in there, we'll be alright.

And in the process? Well, we might just light some fires. Little fires, medium fires and who knows, maybe we might just light a fire so fucking big that we change the world.

Your world.

'No matter what you do, in the beginning it's going to suck, because you suck. But you'll get better, and you'll suck less. And as you keep doing this, eventually you'll suck so little, you'll actually be good.'

—*Garrett J. White*

Fuck yeah.

Onwards.

CHAPTER 2

Dreamers Unite

> *'The only people for me are the mad ones, the ones who are mad to live, mad to talk, mad to be saved, desirous of everything at the same time, the ones who never yawn or say a commonplace thing, but burn, burn, burn like fabulous yellow roman candles exploding like spiders across the stars.'*
>
> *—Jack Kerouac*

We're all dreamers. We've all dreamed. Some do it more than others. Some take it seriously and others think it's childish. Some have decided there's no longer any point. It's silly. It's stupid, why bother?

When we're 5 years old we're actively encouraged to dream and think big and then by our teenage years we're told to grow up and stop daydreaming. Life becomes serious, it's time to become society.

Society: Be yourself.
Society: Not like that.

On my first ever day at school I was asked, as one of the new starts, to stand up in assembly in front of the whole school and share with everyone what I wanted to be when I was older. Three other children stood up alongside me.

I went last.

> Child 1: When I grow up I want to be a hairdresser.
> Child 2: I want to be a train driver.
> Child 3: When I'm older I'm going to be a footballer.
> Me: When I'm bigger I want to be a rhinoceros.

In case you're wondering how that worked out, it hasn't. Turns out when I broke my goal down into manageable chunks and ran it through SMART, it still wasn't doable.

'You can be whatever you want in life,' they tell us.

No, you can't.

Well, you can't always be *exactly* what you want to be. I can't really be a rhinoceros for the simple reason that it's impossible. I'm a human, apparently. Maybe in these modern times I could identify as a rhinoceros? Turns out I can't be a Transformer either. Optimus Prime is out the question. For me certainly, maybe not my son.

But I *could* work with rhinoceroses or I *could* design Transformers for a living, right?

I know this is really obvious, but it's just so simple that millions of people don't see it. We accept something is impossible and we put it down to a silly dream. Or someone else decides for us.

If you think about it there's always a way. This is because we're human beings and we're absolutely fucking awesome. We're born awesome, all of us.

Random fact: Did you know you're born with invisible kneecaps? They literally don't show up in X-rays even though babies definitely do have kneecaps! This is awesome.

Did you know you were built for genius? Actual genius.

I bet some of you reading this are thinking, 'Nope, not me, not a chance, there's no way I'm a genius.'

Likewise, one or two of you might be thinking, 'Well actually, yes I am!'

You have one hundred billion brain cells that make ten thousand connections each at any one time.

This means we are capable of doing stuff. Wee stuff, medium stuff and crazy amounts of big stuff.

It even allows you to produce enough saliva in your lifetime to fill two swimming pools. Absolutely nothing to do with this book but how cool is that?

Your brain is amazing. And just like your intergluteal cleft (Google it...), it's especially amazing when you use it.

There's one particular part of the brain I want to draw your attention to. It's called your imagination. Yes, I know you're an adult and you have heard of it before, but do you really know what it's capable of?

You might just think it allows you to think about stuff differently, but it's your imagination and thoughts that create your future. Think about how magical this makes you – you can see the actual fucking future!

Throughout life you'll hear all sorts of people telling you that 'thoughts become things'. Albert Einstein said, 'Imagination is everything, it is the preview for life's coming attractions.'

It's all too easy to get stuck in life and feel like we're not moving forward but our imaginations allow us to focus on the real life that we want to experience.

But we know life sucks sometimes.

We all have moments in life that we wish had never happened. Death, sadness, sickness, fall outs with friends, that moment you step on Lego or worse, kneel on Lego. The list goes on.

But we also know life is magical sometimes.

Your imagination is what allows this to happen. It allows us to take the mundane and turn it into the magical. It's basically your superpower. Think back to when you were 4 years old and someone handed you a cardboard box. What did you do with it?

Drove it. Flew it. Decorated it. Sailed it. Transformed it. Surfed it. Ate it.

You turned it into anything you wanted.

With your imagination.

I bet you're smiling as you are reading this. Taking a moment to remember what it was like to view the world through the eyes of a 4-year-old reminds us of the joy and wonder the imagination brings.

So, I want to test your imagination right now.

On the opposite page I want you to write a letter to yourself from the 4-year-old you offering you some advice for life. Just what would the 4-year-old you have to say? Go on, give it a bash. This exercise is done best sitting cross-legged with crayons in one hand and Hula Hoops on your fingers. The carton of Ribena is optional, but I suggest sugar free. Just write the first thing that pops into your head. What would the 4-year-old you be telling you to do with your life right now?

I bet it doesn't involve anything to do with social media, Wi-Fi or being a grown up…

Letter from 4-Year-Old Me

So, let's get this right…

We can't be 'anything we want to be' and dreams don't always come true, but with the help of our imagination we can bloody well try our best!

And of course, the world needs dreamers.

There's just one problem: most of us give up on our dreams.

It pained me to write that last sentence. I kinda spewed a little in my own mouth. I wrote it and then deleted it several times. But I'm keeping it in.

Because it's true.

But not all of us. There's a select few of us in the world who don't think of it as silly or childish in any way to chase our dreams. We still allow ourselves to imagine and become excited; it brings us focus and a determination that many others can lose.

I'm a great believer in dreaming. Any dreaming. Day dreaming, dreaming big, lucid dreams, recurring dreams, living your dreams. Just not nightmares – although in attempting to achieve your dreams, you'd better be ready for a few nightmares along the way. We'll deal with them later!

We should all be encouraged to dream big, really big.

Daydream Believer

Like many kids, my dream from a young age was to make it. Well, to be completely honest my dream was simply to be famous. Rock star, comedian, TV presenter – didn't really matter to me. I just wanted to be famous.

I realize now that this is where many of the problems associated with dreaming lie. The concept of 'making it' has no real purpose or meaning to it. But this is a real problem with modern life, there are a fair few people out there building a life for themselves around just this: making it.

But as I got into my early teens the dream had begun to take shape.

I had one eye on going to university, as this was what was expected of me, and one eye set firmly on the world-famous Edinburgh Fringe Festival, the most legendary arts festival in the world.

This all stemmed from my obsession with comedy as a kid. In particular, sketch comedy.

All through my teens I couldn't stop watching Vic Reeves and Bob Mortimer, *Monty Python*, and anything that had Rik Mayall in it. I also loved *Saturday Night Live* and *The Kids in the Hall.* They were different from the norm. Off the wall, surreal nonsense. Crazy characters, wacky costumes and pure silliness. I was drawn to them. I had no idea at the time but I realize now that it gave me a sense of escapism.

Surely I could do what they do? Them and me, weirdos together.

It felt like I'd belong in their world; I'd lie in bed every night playing it out. In my mind I had found the perfect job. There appeared to be a place for me in the world after all.

Others' opinions were not always so positive.

I grew up in the 1990s. The 1990s were awesome, especially if you wanted to be in a band. Don't get me wrong, I love music, and I especially loved music in the 1990s and if I could sing or play a musical instrument I'd absolutely have formed a band. And in my mind we'd have been great. Think KISS meets Green Day meets Queen meets Bowie meets Rolling Stones meets Ramones meets Pink Floyd meets the 1990s. Yup, I've thought about it long and hard; we'd be called Sweet Brioche.

But if you wanted to wear silly dresses, beards, wigs and put on silly voices… not so acceptable. It wasn't cool – yet. So I kept it to myself. I told very few people that I was going to go for it. But this is the key part, I *was* going to go for it. I may only have been a young teenager, but I knew.

'The world needs dreamers and the world needs doers. But above all, the world needs dreamers who do.'

—Sarah Ban Breathnach

This is the bit that really interests me about having a dream. Why do some people dream about something but then do nothing about it? And why do some people dream about something and do everything to make it happen? The latter might not succeed but they'll do everything they can to try. Perhaps that's why the former don't pursue their dream, maybe the fear of failure is enough to put some of us off? Perhaps it's the fear of what others will think?

I worried about what others would say and think but the desire to live my dream was greater. I needed to 'make it'. Whatever that meant…

So, I decided to give it a go.

Now, for the purposes of 'scene setting', I need to share a little of my comedy journey with you. It's not a case of 'Hey readers, check out what I achieved,' it's more a case of 'Hey readers, check out the awesome adventure I went on where I totally nearly made it but totally didn't make it, and it hurt for a very long time but years later as I put things into perspective I realized I totally did make it…just in other ways.'

That last sentence may not make good grammatical sense, but I hope you get the gist of it.

OK, stay with me…

My first Edinburgh Fringe was way back in 2000 as one half of a double act known as Gav 'n' Rolls. Rolls was my best friend, the best friend I ever had. We grew up together, inseparable and with a shared love of all things silly. Rolls is to this day the funniest human I've ever met in my life. There is no one else in the world that has made me laugh as much as this dude. To make it even better, he also has a beautiful soul. One of the good guys.

We were about 20 years old and had absolutely no idea what we were doing. No performing experience, no background in theatre and no showbiz parents who had been there before us. But we went for it. Days spent writing and rehearsing. Hours and hours spent pacing the cobbled streets of Edinburgh, handing out thousands of flyers to potential audience members, trying to convince even just one person to come and see our first ever full hour of comedy.

There were no smart phones, so we didn't have the power of Facebook or Twitter. This required us to turn up fully.

'*You* guys are doing comedy?' they asked regularly, with puzzled faces.

We had no money and absolutely zero reputation, so we had to just get ourselves out there and give it everything we had. And at 3 p.m. every single day we took to a tiny stage in the corner of a basement in a pub (WJ Christie's) in the Grassmarket, Edinburgh.

Our biggest audience that year was 36. Our smallest was 1. And we had 2 'no show' days, as no one turned up.

This hurt. A lot.

We kept going.

Of course, we didn't live in Edinburgh and had nowhere to stay for the month. The plan was to ask people in the audience each day if they wanted us to live with them, for free, for four weeks. This was either crazy or genius. And in the meantime we had Rolls's mum's car and two sleeping bags as back up! We also had huge belief in humanity and on day one, among our huge audience of 11, we met Grant and Polly who not only enjoyed our show but offered us a place to stay.

This blew our minds. They enjoyed *our* show *and* asked if we wanted to crash at their place! Friends for life and we still owe them both big time.

How awesome are humans and, of course, that's the Fringe for you!

Our first Edinburgh Fringe was incredible. In some people's minds our run that year could be described as a massive flop, a huge failure. Barely anyone turned up and we didn't make a penny. No one wrote about us and no one got excited.

No one gave a shit. Except us. We got excited. We gave a fuck.

I mentioned in the previous chapter that everything boils down to thinking. We have a choice, always. We chose to see our experience as a success. We chose to get excited. We chose to care.

We were just so thankful for the whole experience. We stood at the door after each show and thanked every single audience member for coming as we shook their hands. We mixed and performed with many other new acts, some of whom have gone on to become household names.

And that's part of the lure of course, you *might* make it. Every year there are two or three acts whose stars align and it happens. Sometimes on a scale that many only ever dream of. And that, remember, had always been my dream.

To make it. Again, whatever that even means.

But that's just it. *Everyone* in the Fringe is a dreamer. We're all dreaming of the same thing. Packed out venues, queues all the way down the street, roars of laughter, five star reviews and rubbing shoulders with your heroes. And if you work hard, give it everything and don't act like a dick then it *might* actually happen.

Note In life some proper dicks do make it, unfortunately, and some proper good people turn into massive dicks…

We put ourselves out there, taking on every gig we could, travelling the length and breadth of the country sharing our minds with anyone who would listen.

In a short space of time it took us around the world. In 2002, we completed a successful run at the Melbourne International Comedy Festival in Australia. Shit was getting real. The dream was coming true. This was it.

Except it wasn't it.

After a year living out of a suitcase, performing at some of the biggest festivals in the world, for so many reasons that I still don't fully understand, it all came to an end.

It was over.

From what in my mind felt like a great height, I fell hard.

For the first time in my life I felt down. Like, really down. I'm very reluctant to use the word 'depressed' here because I didn't seek professional help and it's not a subject to fuck about with. But I was depressed. I know that now but at the time as I lay in my bed crying myself to sleep every night, I didn't have a clue what was wrong with me. I just put it down to being very, very sad. I was so sad I smelled of sadness. The dream was over. Gone. And my best friend in the whole world had decided on another path. Like all good double acts, we drifted, and this was the hardest part. The constant focus on 'making it' had ultimately driven a wedge between me and the most important friend I've ever had.

Twenty-two years old and the fun had gone. Life felt kinda shit.

In 2003, I decided to get a job at the Edinburgh Fringe working for legendary theatre company Gilded Balloon. I figured it would allow me to keep a 'foot in the door' of the comedy world. They put me in charge of running 'The Caves', a venue that would go on to mean more to me than any other venue in the world. Apart from Troon Town Hall, of course (December 2000), but that's a whole other story for a whole other book. Gilded Balloon had dozens of shows on in The Caves that year, but two in particular will stick in my mind forever.

Stick with me here, reader, there's some key learning coming up...

Firstly, I want to mention 'Slaughterhouse Live'. They were on in the Big Cave, a venue that is quite literally a cave. It holds 150 people and has an extraordinary atmosphere. This show inspired me and my comedy more than any other show I've ever seen at the Fringe.

'Normality is a paved road: It's comfortable to walk, but no flowers grow.'

—Vincent van Gogh

Five guys working together to create a world that was entirely their own. Clever, silly, horrific, disgusting, surreal and utterly, utterly hilarious. Still to this day the best and funniest show I have ever seen. To quote their Fringe poster that year, Slaughterhouse Live were 'so wrong it's right'. It was very Gav 'n' Rolls. High energy, in-your-face humour. Why they didn't have TV execs queuing to sign them up I'll never know.

With Gav 'n' Rolls having come to a very difficult end, Slaughterhouse Live was the one show that picked me up and gave me the belief that one day I'd have my chance once again. Maybe one day I'd play the Big Cave to a full house like them. I was, for the first time in months, feeling inspired again.

Secondly, a fairly new act called 'Flight of the Conchords' were also playing the big stage in The Caves that year. I hadn't heard too much about them other than their 2002 Fringe had been quite good. I saw something happen that year that blew my mind. Right from the start, these two guys from New Zealand had a packed-out venue, queues all the way down the street, five star reviews and some of the biggest names in comedy clambering for a ticket and in some cases (a very famous TV comedian who will remain nameless) *desperate* to be their friend. It was very clear to me that Flight of the

Conchords would go on to become a global phenomenon. I saw it happen. It was possible, but couldn't be further from what I had experienced just a few years earlier with Rolls.

But the thing that struck me the most about both Slaughterhouse Live and Flight of the Conchords was not the fact their shows were fucking great but the fact they were/are such nice guys. All of them. Down to earth. Lovely. No ego. A delight to talk to. Helpful. Encouraging. Who better to spend a month in a cave with?

The other thing that appealed to me was the fact they were in it together. Conchords as a double act and Slaughterhouse as a five-piece. Each act a team. Bouncing ideas off each other, sharing the highs and, of course, the lows. A true connection, a friendship. No one better than the other.

How do you find that in others? The types of people that it all just clicks with, when it's just meant to be. I'll say it until the day I die, Gav 'n' Rolls had it. We could've and should've been huge. But whilst we had some unbelievable times it simply wasn't meant to be. It took me over ten years to accept that.

Ten years.

But I learned that just like people, dreams can change. Dreams do change. Sometimes – again, like people – they must. And that's OK.

Fast forward to Edinburgh Fringe 2012. I had thrown myself back in. Along with a magician and a mind reader, I was now part of a three-piece act known as 'The Colour Ham'. A sketch magic show. A what, I hear you ask?! Three very different performers from very different backgrounds creating something entirely new. Almost ten years of an age gap between oldest and youngest.

On paper our show simply should not have worked.

Our show was rejected by all the major Fringe venues except one, 'Just the Tonic', who took a punt. Due to other commitments we could only commit to the first 11 nights. It just so happened they had a slot available for those 11 nights. At 9 p.m. In The Caves. The Big Cave. THE BIG CAVE. It was like it was meant to be and although this time we knew a little bit more about what we were doing, we were still winging it.

Just simply going for it. I realized this is when I'm at my happiest. There's an idea, no plan and I'm just simply going for it. With other amazing people.

The Colour Ham went on to play the Big Cave three years in a row at the Fringe. We had a packed venue, sold out pretty much every night, won awards and performed for the BBC.

It took ten years.

'They came out of nowhere,' said one reviewer.

Ten fucking years.

There were queues all the way down the street, five-star reviews, and we rubbed shoulders with our heroes. We had the team, the connection, that thing that Gav 'n' Rolls, Slaughterhouse and Conchords all had. Everything I had dreamed of was coming true. Finally.

'I always did something I was a little not ready to do. I think that's how you grow. When there's that moment of, "Wow, I'm not really sure I can do this," and you push through those moments, that's when you have a breakthrough.'

—Marissa Mayer

I used to dream that one day people would write about us. I used to imagine 15-year-olds sitting in their bedrooms reading the reviews of *my* show, inspiring *them* to create their own.

I used to write imaginary reviews, but now people were writing about *us*. People like writer Vonny Moyes who wrote things like this…

(Please read the whole review, dear reader.)

> Taking refuge from a dreich Friday, I drink coffee with a magician, a mentalist and a comedian. An unusual coterie; these lot tend to move in their own herds. As an outsider looking in, it seems remarkable they're even friends, let alone creating something as a unit. And not just creating – after sell-out runs at two Fringes, five-star reviews they've earned a prestigious residency at The Stand, Glasgow; a recognised barometer of comedy talent. They've conceived something quite special, and unlike anything you've seen before.
>
> Kevin, Colin and Gavin – a reformed physicist, ex-forensic scientist and a one-time primary school teacher are The Colour Ham. Sounding part Discworld, part Python, I question the name, but am denied the anecdote for now.
>
> These three are on a mission to boldly reclaim laughter. To reinvent the comedy show. To take what you think you know about magic, comedy and mentalism, destroy it and rearrange it in a way that just hasn't been done yet. They'll contact your dead pets, re-enact your first kiss, and rewrite Pinocchio through the medium of a military crotch. All three are keen to talk, and I'm soon initiated into their very particular brand of nonsense. The sort of thing

that's comfortingly reminiscent of the best of Vic and Bob, yet distinctly their own. The thing that strikes me most about them is just how much they believe in what they're doing. Of course, everyone wants to hit it big. Every person who's ever thought 'fuck it, I'm doing this' and defiantly chased a dream has believed they were good enough. Though, somehow, there's almost a lightbulb moment here. A glimpse of something indescribable that makes you think they might just be on to something.

They are warm, and passionate. All three are instantly likeable; the bond between them is brotherly and I chuckle as they comfortably tear one another apart. Separately, they'd do well; Kevin and Colin already have their disciples from their forays in the magic world, as does Gav from his previous incarnation as a stand-up. What's really interesting is that despite a decent chance at self-derived success, they're doing this together. Eschewing the easier option in favour of an idea. A spark of ingenuity. That doesn't happen so much. We're a world away from the nebulous 80s that hit us with more alternative comedy than we could handle. Since then things have mellowed, so it's really exciting to catch something that rejects the status quo, and is proud to be completely unique.

These days, it's not enough to just stand on stage and do a variation on a theme we've all seen a hundred times, from a hundred different acts. The only way anyone can hope of connecting with an audience these days is to reach out – often literally – and grab them. You've really got to scream with every fibre of your being for anyone to take the blindest bit of notice. Then, you've got to hold their attention.

Let's just admit it; we're all bored. We need something new, even if we don't quite know what that is yet. 'The secret to humour is

> surprise,' Aristotle once said. It's the not-so-secret ingredient. The Colour Ham know this, and are juicing it. Maybe this is what we all need? A real surprise. A chance to indulge that irreverent idiocy we've absent-mindedly neglected in recent times. These three are pioneering a new standard of funny, and forging something memorable; the sort of thing you'll tell your friends about.
>
> There's no doubt that they want it enough; the truth of it is that we need them as much as they need us. We're not going to find the antidote to modern living on telly; not while the likes of panel shows and Britain's Got Talent have set the bar for acceptable mediocrity. We, intrepid thrill-seekers, must go out and find the cure ourselves. We need to lighten up. To remember that silliness is good for the soul. The Colour Ham want to make you happier for the cost of a few quid. Who can say no to that? The only thing for it is to ditch your sensibilities. Put on your coat and step out. Grab a bite, actually see a show. Have this crafted, irreplicable experience. And hey, you just might enjoy it.
>
> Comedy is the new rock and roll, folks, and this band are on the verge of something great. See them while the tickets are still cheap.
>
> Reproduced with kind permission of *The Skinny*

What a review! It blows my mind every time I read it.

She saw it. She saw what I had seen years before in all my comedy heroes. Better still, she compared us to them. The passion, the togetherness, the bond, the 'fuck it' attitude, the rejection of the status quo. The kindness, the importance of fun and silliness, the desire to brighten the world, to surprise, to create excitement. We were 'making it'.

It was the dream review.

The dream was coming true.

And then guess what?

It ended.

Just as quickly as it all began.

Devastated.

Again.

One year later, in 2015, for the last time ever, we performed together at the Edinburgh Fringe. This was to be our fourth and final Fringe together.

So many reasons why. Busyness, family commitments, external influences, business commitments and ego to name a few...

On stage the fun was still there, off stage it wasn't. This had gone some time before. This is how I knew it was coming to an end.

I can't speak for the other guys but for me, three best friends having the time of their lives now felt like three colleagues vying for the centre spot on the posters.

Three incredibly close friends now felt like three distant and very busy acquaintances struggling to find the time for each other.

Three mates without a care in the world, going for it and following their hearts, now worrying about reputations, listening to the 'guiding' voices of others, now ruled by their heads.

'Making it' seemed to have got in the way yet again…

Once more I found myself feeling very very down. The smell of sadness lingered once again.

After years of performing and working as part of this extraordinary festival I find myself not involved these days. And it feels very strange. I've moved on to different things and we've all had success. Part of me is absolutely delighted. The Fringe is exhausting, stressful, difficult and full of wankers. I'm now able to go see shows, and most importantly see my family, and August no longer costs me an absolute fortune.

But I can't lie, the other part of me is heartbroken. All those years working so hard to create something that made people laugh until they cried. One review read 'I laughed so hard I nearly shat.' I'm proud of that one.

The Fringe is exhilarating, it's magical, it's bloody wonderful. Some of my happiest times were on stage at the Fringe with The Colour Ham and I miss it. I miss performing. I miss the buzz. I miss being in that moment on stage with the team when you don't even need to say anything, you just know what each other is thinking. That moment when the audience know and you know that something really special is happening there and then between real friends and it's pure magic. I miss that.

I miss my best friends.

Colin, Kevin and, of course, Rolls. I love you all.

But I did it. *We* did it.

I gave it my all and I rocked the fuck out. *We* rocked the fuck out and people nearly shat themselves – there's a legacy to be proud of…

The Edinburgh Fringe is an absolute beast. It's not everyone's idea of a dream. But like every dream, it shouldn't be feared but respected.

Dreams can make *and* break you. But it's a hell of a ride. To anyone who's thinking about dropping everything and going for it, then please do.

'Never let go of that fiery sadness called desire.'

—Patti Smith

No matter what your dream is, if you decide to go for it, then give it everything. It might just lead to the most extraordinary adventure. It might all come crashing down around you but don't let it turn you into a dick and whatever you do, remember those who inspired you, remain thankful and always *always* remember your friends who were there at the start. One day you might just stop and realize you forgot all about the ones who gave a shit.

'If you sit on a shelf for the rest of your life, you'll never find out.'

—Woody, Toy Story 4

And remember, dreams *can* change.

Sometimes they have to.

To new dreams.

CHAPTER 3

Never Be Afraid of Your Own Style

'It's okay to begin your story today. Those mistakes you've made along the way are lessons, not failures. You were meant to get back up and find a way that resonates with you. There is no expiration date to reinventing yourself.'

—Anon

My other big passion in life is teaching. And in amongst all my years of writing and performing I managed to bag myself an honours degree in primary school teaching.

Teaching and live stand-up are essentially the same thing, you need to capture your audience quickly and take them on the most wonderful journey you possibly can.

I am always amazed at how many people tell me they could never be a teacher and how awful it must be working with little kids all day!

Eh, have you ever worked with *adults* all day? Adults are the worst kind of children.

I've learned more working with children than I ever have with adults, particularly about myself. I have been more inspired by children under the age of ten than I ever have been by adults.

And I've had more fun working with kids, fact.

Their resilience, mindset, character, creativity and ability to bounce forward, to move on when the time is right is not wasted on me. Kids rarely hold grudges; well-known Disney movies have played their role beautifully in teaching a generation to Let It Go. The Beatles taught the previous generation to Let It Be. I'm not entirely sure which is best or if they are the same. I'll let you decide.

Even the way young kids deal with each other is magnificent. The following is a genuine conversation between two young nursery kids aged three, standing around the sandpit.

> Child 1: We're not friends anymore.
> Child 2: I know.

Done! That's it, it's over. No weirdness, wasn't even slightly uncomfortable.

Seven minutes later, same two kids standing around the same sandpit.

> Child 1: Wanna be best friends again?
> Child 2: Yes I do, LET'S DIG!

Done! It's back on. We've dealt with our issues and we've made it all lovely again.

It's never as easy when we're adults. When shit goes wrong it hurts. It hurts for young people, too, but in these moments as kids we are always asked about what we've learned, what we've gained and what's the lesson. Kids are often great at articulating this because we teach them how to accept what's happened, learn from the negatives and move on.

But as adults we just seem to unlearn all of this. We wallow, we go weird, we don't like it. We're told by loved ones to just be positive about it, to put things in perspective. Let's be honest, being told to put things in perspective is shit advice. So we bitch, we moan, we complain.

Through all the work I do in the world of education and the incredible young people I meet, I am forever reminded of the importance of learning. But also, learning to learn. Making time for learning and to embrace it.

A child's ability and willingness to learn from situations blows my mind daily. They remind me that learning is so much more than education. Learning is a constant process which involves learning to live, to learn, to socialize and to behave. To keep learning is key.

Highs and lows are staple in life. What we learn from them is key and the action we take is what makes the difference. When I give time to learning I notice a real shift in my confidence; when I'm down it lifts my levels of happiness. Learning is so much more than education and financial success. It can be used to truly influence life in the most positive ways.

I think most of us are open to learning, I'm just not sure we're all entirely open to being taught!

Here's some shit that life has taught me…

1. You Don't Have to Make It to Make It

'What do you want to be when you're older?'

'I'm going to make it!'

'In what?'

'Dunno.'

The desire to 'make it' is a popular dream. It pollutes teenage minds and bedrooms the world over. It's a hunger shared by millions. But what stipulates 'making it' and where does it end?

Is it when you have it all? Whoever you are, being a rock star in every single area of your life is an unattainable goal and creates an undue amount of pressure.

That's part of the problem. It doesn't end. The goal of 'making it' is a never-ending struggle with ever-changing goalposts. It drains us of all our energy and over time deletes many a friendship as we don our blinkers in search of the holy grail.

I have very few friends. Don't get me wrong, I have wonderful friends but there's not many of them. Real ones anyway. I know for a fact there are people no longer in my life because I was simply too busy 'making it'. FFS.

To be able to say 'I've made it' at the expense of true happiness, friendship and love is one of life's great mysteries and yet it lures millions into its lifelong chase.

Instead of trying to 'make it', work out what 'making it' actually means to you. Is it to produce a body of work you are proud of? Is it to have a house? A family? To run your own business?

But is it the end result or is it more about becoming a better person, learning, making a difference, being happy or having fantastic experiences? Work it out for the sake of your own happiness because the goal of 'making it' doesn't cut it, nor does it end. Ever.

2. We All Need a Hero

Nineteenth-century historian Thomas Carlyle once observed that 'Society is founded on hero-worship.' Now, whether you agree with this or not, based on my own experiences and observations I definitely believe that to this day society still strives to ensure those who embody the best values of our culture are held up as objects of admiration. Whether we get this right or not is a whole other conversation. I mean, just take a look at the news FFS.

Scott Labarge writes that we need heroes because 'they define the limits of our aspirations'. But of course we're all different and my idea of a hero will be very different to the next person. And if it's true that we define our ideals by the heroes we choose then there's a good chance that you and I will be quite different with a very different sense of what human awesomeness actually involves.

'One day, whether you are 14, 28 or 65, you will stumble upon someone who will start a fire in you that cannot die.'

—Beau Taplin

My heroes involve rock stars (mainly dead ones), writers, rugby players, comedians and my parents. If yours is Donald Trump, Jesus or Kim Kardashian then it's very likely you and I will see the world a touch differently.

But that's OK. Kind of…

My heroes have always been people I admire and wish to emulate. Their achievements, performances, scripts, lyrics, humour and stories gave me a sense of possibility. They helped me to define the limits of my aspirations. They made me feel excited, like there was a place in the world for someone like me. My heroes gave me hope and a sense of belonging. They still do.

Find your hero and allow yourself to be inspired by them.

3. Take Part

Life tells us from a young age that it's the taking part that counts. I'm not sure if many people believe this to be true; for most, the winning is still a priority. In competitive sport I get it. It's absolutely about the winning. In non-competitive sports then I absolutely agree that we can play for fun, it's good for us, it's fun and it can be social.

As a business owner I also understand competition. I understand why companies and their leadership want to be number one. But I also feel more comfortable working *with* others. Just a few years ago, one of our 'competitors' wrote a letter to literally every single one of our clients criticizing our business, telling them they were wasting their money using our services. Who does this? This is wrong on so many levels but we'll go with 'professionally' and 'morally' for now. Their defence was 'Well, business is business.'

Mega lolz.

But let's just imagine it was true and it really is the taking part that counts. What if there was room for everyone? What if – as long as we're all in it for the right reason – we can share the space and make a bigger difference, together? In the case of our 'competitor' mentioned above, we both work in schools for fuck's sake. We both want to help children to be more resilient and create positive futures. What if I'm fully booked up and an enquiry comes in that we simply cannot fulfil, I was able to say to the client, 'Give these folks a call, they're magic.'

I know there are businesses that exist who do this. But not many. And I understand you're only going to recommend others who you believe to be excellent. But I like the sound and feel of this. The reality is that within business, for all the wonderful, purpose-led, values-driven individuals out there, there are just too many cliques and too many egos.

Much like life. But what if it were different?

What if we didn't just reward winning? What if we paid more attention to the 'taking part'? The 'doing', the 'trying' or even the 'not winning'? The 'failing'?

I'm not a subscriber to the 'Let's not dish out medals on sports day as everyone's a winner' mentality. If you're the best then you should absolutely win.

But what if you're the best at being 4th? Imagine being 4th best in the whole fucking world at something but you don't get anything for it.

3rd = medals and flowers. 4th = nowt.

Or the best at being shit at running? Should there be a prize for this? OK, I'm being facetious now but life is for taking part. Turning up, getting stuck in, involved. But you don't need to be the best. You don't need to win. We can however enjoy living, enjoy being 'in' rather than 'out'.

What about having the 4th best beard in the world? Never mind this 1st, 2nd or 3rd best beard nonsense, 4th best beard is where it's at.

Random, huh?

Read on…

In 2007, I entered the World Moustache and Beard Championships. Yes, it's true, this is actually a thing that exists. Men (and occasionally women) from all over the world spend years growing, shaping, taming, sculpting and moulding their facial whiskers, and every two years they gather somewhere in the world to celebrate the best of the best.

I only found out by chance about the World Moustache and Beard Championships 90 days before the actual competition and decided to enter. But there was a problem. I didn't have a moustache or a beard.

So, without any egging on from anyone, I filled in the forms and let the growing begin. I entered a category called 'Partial Beard Freestyle'. Again, this is actually a thing.

I set myself the following challenge:

- No shaving for 90 days
- Style it the night before the competition
- Turn up

For 90 days, slowly but surely my beard began to take on a life of its own and before I knew it, it looked like a giant loaf of wholemeal bread had made home on my face.

People laughed, others pointed. Occasionally, I was met with shouts of 'Hey Chewbacca', 'hairy face' and my particular favourite, 'How many birds live in there?'

Games of 'How Many Things Can You Hide in Gav's Beard?' became a regular fixture. And just in case anyone is wondering…17 is the record. Often people would poke fun at my ever-growing facial forest of fuzz. I, however, kept on growing.

The 90 days dragged on…

On the eve of the World Moustache and Beard Championships I drove for nine hours and in line with the original plan, in my hotel, I styled my beard.

The initial plan had been to style my beard into the word 'beard' but I was concerned that because I was doing it in the mirror the result may in fact read 'bread'.

So a last minute change of plan resulted in an epic sweeping moustache/sideburn combo with an enormous chin-talon of awesomeness. Photos do exist.

I donned my kilt and headed off to represent Scotland in the most prestigious Moustache and Beard competition in the world. When I turned up I couldn't believe how many other contestants there were. Over 300 beard growers from all over the world had arrived. Beards down to the floor, spikey beards, curly beards, even beards in the shape of London Bridge. Every single style, shape, size you could imagine and more.

Over the next three hours a strange combo of London Fashion Week and Crufts for humans proceeded to unfold. Two thousand people turned up to watch. Yes, 2000 people left their homes to look at beards and moustaches.

My name was called and I took to the stage, my facial masterpiece receiving thunderous applause.

That day I came 4th in the world. You will rarely meet anyone else in life who has achieved such a thing.

Throughout this story you have probably been wondering why on earth I or anyone else would have given the time and energy to such a bizarre undertaking?

It's simple.

Because I can. I wanted to take part.

It may be a bit different from the norm, but hey, normal is boring right? It might be a bit weird, but hey, weird is also exciting right?

It's no different to why people play football, sing, dance, draw, build and so on.

Because they can.

You don't even have to be the best but you can still be a part of something. You can still compete. You can still have fun.

It's amazing when you find something that's your thing. Something you can get into and be bothered about.

And who knows, you might even come 4th in the world.

I See You

It's a time of badges, certificates, medals, trophies, recognition, awards, prizes and 'seeing' of high achievement. We love seeing the kids that shine at this time of year – a big high heartfelt round of applause to you. You so deserve it for the effort you have put in… But this message is for the kids that didn't get called up for any of the above; I SEE YOU.

To the child that conquered their fear of heights or sleeping in the dark, or riding a bike without training wheels or sleeping out for the night for the first time this year, I SEE YOU.

To the child that managed to resolve more conflict than they started this year, to the child that learnt to say the impossible: 'I'm sorry', and to the child that walked away from the fighting instead of getting involved, I SEE YOU.

To the child for whom school is a huge struggle, you get up every day and you go, I SEE YOU.

To the child that battled all year with the maths, or reading, or concentration, or speaking out in class, or learning their words, but persevered anyway, I SEE YOU.

To the child that found the kindness in their heart to reach out in any way to another person or to an animal in need or in pain, I SEE YOU.

To the child that learnt to give and to share for the first time this year and even found joy in these, I SEE YOU.

To the child that battles to make friends and to be social, you made new friends this year and for that, I SEE YOU.

To the child who wanted so much to please, but was just out of sight of an adult who perhaps was too busy or too distracted, I SEE YOU.

To the child who lost a friend or a loved one this year, but carried on every day bravely even though their heart ached, I SEE YOU.

To the brave parents that try every day to do the best for their kids, I SEE YOU.

May you and your children revel in small but significant victories that you have both experienced this year, as I will with my beautiful children. For every year there is progress and growth, we don't need a podium or handshake or a hall of applause to be seen. I SEE YOU.

Written by Colleen Wilson. www.facebook.com/ContemporaryParenting/; www.facebook.com/colleenwilsoncoach/. Reproduced with permission.

4. Jumpers for Goalposts

Just about every single self-help, personal development–type book on the planet covers goal setting. I'm choosing not to. Well, I'm going to mention stuff about goals but I'm not going to share any one particular technique. For me it's simple: just fucking set some, work hard at them and don't make them impossible.

As I've mentioned, 'To make it' is a shit goal. It doesn't mean anything, it's not measurable and it just doesn't end.

We all know that setting goals makes a huge contribution to the success of an individual or a team. It's fairly common knowledge that most successful people are goal-orientated. We all know that they take time to identify what it is that they want and then build up a really clear and detailed picture of what achieving the goal will look and feel like. They then break it down into small manageable chunks and take regular action to move towards their goal. We know this, right? We've been taught this since school.

We know, we know, we know, we know.

So, if it's this goddamn obvious then why aren't we all doing it? Why aren't we all achieving our dreams and living the life we've envisioned for ourselves. Because 'going for it' scares us and requires a shitload of hard work, effort and energy. And this in turn requires a growth mindset.

There's going to be a lot of knockbacks, closed doors and rejection. Failure almost certainly will rear its beautiful head. Beautiful? Yes, in all its glory it is simply stunning. It's a gift. It just doesn't feel like it at the time.

5. The Long Lost Art of Giving a Fuck

Giving a fuck is for life, not just for Christmas.

But, we've not got unlimited fucks and we need to direct them to the stuff that truly matters.

I wonder if many of you reading this remember what it used to be like before the 'Look at all the fucks I give' movement began?

It's become a thing. Nowadays there are books, courses, podcasts, apps and retreats all designed to help teach us to give less fucks. Or at best, zero fucks at all.

Let this sink in…

You can pay thousands of pounds to go on a retreat to teach you how to give less fucks. WTF?

'Giving no fucks' is currently cool. It's in and many influencers (ironically, I don't give a fuck about anyone who calls themselves an 'influencer'. Or 'guru' for that matter) are attempting to teach us that in this modern day and age we will get further, all be more successful and all be happier if we simply adopt the attitude of 'I don't give a fuck'.

I get it. I get that this all started as a fashionable, hipster kind of way of delivering the same inspirational messages that have always been delivered, just in a more marketable way. The core message being that we need to focus on the good stuff and not worry and stress about the stuff that doesn't matter. Again, I get it. I agree.

But it's gone too far. We have people who give a fuck about not giving a fuck. All their fucks are then given to being the person who just doesn't care.

We must give a fuck. And we must get better at it.

Look at the world right now. There are simply not enough fucks being given. The whole planet appears to be doomed for the very reason that some people simply don't have any more fucks to give.

Mark Manson absolutely nails it with his book *The Subtle Art of Not Giving a Fuck.* He writes

> You and everyone you know are going to be dead soon. And in the short amount of time between here and there, you have a limited number of fucks to give. Very few, in fact. And if you go around giving a fuck about everything and everyone without conscious thought or choice—well, then you're going to get fucked.

However, whilst I absolutely agree that our fucks need to be directed towards the stuff that matters, I believe we can squeeze out a few more though. We've got it in us and the world needs it.

I can tell you right now, proudly and unapologetically, I give a fuck. A great big fuckity fuck. I really do!

I give a fuck about me, my health, my family, my friends, my work, my whole life and the whole world. I don't claim to be an expert in anything, I'm not particularly skilled at anything but the journey that life has taken me on is simply down to the fact I give a fuck about making a difference. I want everyone to be happy.

This is very simple. You either give a fuck about you and your life or you don't, there's no in between. There are many things in this world that you can take great pleasure from ignoring. You don't *have* to care about almost everything in the world if you don't want to.

Maybe I care about too many things, maybe I overthink too many things, maybe I just care too much. But maybe that's my thing…

Manson basically says you should save your fucks for magical shit. Trust me. Identify all the magical shit, the stuff you're passionate about, that give you purpose and give all the fucks you have to give and watch your life transform.

DO NOT READ THE NEXT SENTENCE

YOU LITTLE REBEL. I LIKE YOU.

6. Don't Be a Dick

'A dickhead makes everything about them.'

—*Gilbert Enoka*

To be? or not to be…a dick? That is the question, the everyday struggle for so many. We know the answer and yet some choose differently from others.

When I was 19 years old I got a holiday job working for a large well-known high street clothing store. For many reasons, I won't give you the store's name, so let's go with NEXT. Oops.

First day. I arrived suited and booted ready to make an impact. I wore my best shirt, my best trousers and my best shoes. I wanted to make a great first impression.

I arrived nice and early, met the team and was instructed that my first task would be to restock the men's shirts on the shop floor.

Perfect. Nice, simple task. Take the shirts out the box, slide them into the correct spaces on the wall ensuring that the sizes are in order. I can do this.

First shirt needed to be slotted into the lowest space on the shelf. To be clear, the lowest space was pretty much on the floor, 2 inches above to be exact.

So, in order to put the shirt into the slot I would need to bend/crouch down to reach it.

I took the shirt, I bent down. My trousers tore.

I can still hear the noise.

Now, just to provide a little more detail here…

When I say they tore, I don't mean a little tear at the seams that goes unnoticed. I mean the biggest kind of tear that can't *not* be seen. The kind of tear that once you've seen it, you can't unsee it. The kind of tear that had I not been wearing underwear, quite simply and to put it bluntly my balls would have fallen out for all to see.

In simpler terms, there was a draught.

It was the kind of tear you simply don't have on view when working in a clothing store. Or any store.

This was bad.

First day in a new job. First five minutes into the first day of a new job and my ass was hanging out my trousers. I'm having a wee chuckle to myself as I write this but at the time it wasn't so funny. I kinda panicked a little. First impressions and all…

I hatched a plan.

Speak to the boss, do the right thing, tell her what's happened and provide a solution.

My solution was simple: take a new pair of trousers off the rail in the store and pay for them. Or take it out of my wages. It makes sense, right? I'm working in a clothes store; they sell men's trousers. Easy.

The walk from the scene of the accident to my new boss's office would have made for great modern day YouTube viewing. I had to cross the entire shop floor, weaving in and out of both customers and clothing rails trying my best not to reveal what had happened.

I pirouetted my way round the shirts, Vogued through the suits, Time Warped past the shoes, Loco-motioned under the belts, Beyoncé'd my way down the escalator, Moonwalked, Macarena'd and with a bright red face 'Gangnammed-before-it-was-even-invented' my way into the boss's office.

'You have to love dancing to stick to it. It gives you nothing back, no manuscripts to store away, no paintings to show on walls and maybe hang in museums, no poems to be printed and sold, nothing but that single fleeting moment when you feel alive.'

—Merce Cunningham

'Gavin', she said, 'how's the first day going?'

'Well, it's funny you should ask.'

She looked very serious.

'So, it's a little bit embarrassing, I've had a wee accident.'

Her stare hardened.

'But it's easily fixed.'

Her stare was now at Rambo level.

'So, you won't believe this, but as I put the first shirt on the shelf my trousers tore.'

She didn't even flinch.

Surely she should be pissing herself laughing.

Nothing.

'But I have an idea.'

Nothing.

'I'll quickly grab a pair of trousers off the rail and pay for them either today, tomorrow or you can take it out of my wages.'

She raised an eyebrow, still no laughter, not even a tiny little side smile.

She began to speak…

'I have some safety pins. You could turn your trousers inside out and safety pin them. That will do the job I'm sure.'

I proceeded to have one of those moments where you aren't quite sure if the other person is being serious or having a joke at your expense because in this type of situation it fully deserves a joke. I was fully ready to have the utter piss taken out of me and forever more be *that* guy!

So I did what we all do in those moments, I kind of pointed and smiled as if to say, 'You're kidding right?'

Nothing.

In my mind I'm thinking 'This must be a joke. It's a fucking clothes shop. They have trousers. I can buy trousers. I can wear my new trousers.'

Still nothing.

'So…I can't just go and get new trousers?'

'How about you just go home, Gavin?'

WTF?

'Really?'

'Yup. Take the day off and we'll probably just have you working in the stock room from now on.'

'Blowing out someone else's flame won't make yours shine brighter. Remember that.'

—Anon

'You're serious, right? I've to go home and not just buy new trousers in the shop that I am currently working in? That sells trousers. For men. Here. In this shop right now.'

Nothing.

Now, you might be wondering why I'm sharing this story with you in this book. Where's the learning point, where's the big underlying inspirational message?

We'll, it's this…

Some people are dicks.

Simple.

And in my story, my boss proved herself to be a dick. She was being a dick. And I should've told her she was being a dick. I was trying to be as professional about it as possible. It was an accident, a rather embarrassing one at that. But she chose to be a dick about it.

You see, the thing is I believe we can *all* be dicks from time to time. But I also believe we all know when we're being a dick. We just know, right? When you're being a dick there is a voice in your head telling you that you're being a dick. It's telling you you're a dick. You are a dick and you know it.

Being a dick is like sitting your driving theory test. We all know the answer, but still, some fail. We know not to be a dick but sometimes we're just dicks.

So don't be a dick. If you know you're being a dick, stop it. She knew she was being a dick and yet she kept being a dick.

It's time to stop being a dick.

'Some people will only like you if you fit inside their box. Don't be afraid to shove that box up their ass.'

—Anon

As Bernard M. Baruch said,

'Be who you are and say what you feel because those who mind don't matter and those who matter don't mind.'

What should I have said to her in that moment? There were many options. I said nothing.

I thought to myself, 'Don't be a dick'. So I wasn't a dick.

I smiled and I left.

I've always wondered if she watched the CCTV back after I'd left. If she did she'd have seen some of the finest moves ever to be witnessed and she'd have realized I had skills she'd never even heard of.

Asshole.

You're never too important to be nice to people.

7. Ask for Help

'In the beginning of life, when we are infants, we need others to survive, right? And at the end of life, when you get like me, you need others to survive, right? But here's the secret: In between, we need others as well.'

—Morrie Schwartz

Perhaps more importantly, accept it. As kids we're brilliant at this. We're naturally skilled at asking for help when we need it, but we seem to unlearn this life changing skill the busier and more engrossed in 'making it' we become. Many of us adults need to relearn the art of asking for help. You don't have to be the one that does it all, start accepting you're only one person. Once you get it in your head that you are worthy of the luxury of having help from others, your world will open up, allowing you more time to do things that inspire you and, subsequently, those around you. And perhaps more so, we need to get better at accepting help. It doesn't make us weak, in fact it's quite the opposite. It makes us stronger. Better even, at being human. And we need more of this.

'By reaching out, more comes back than you can possibly imagine.'

—Christopher Reeve

8. Arrive Alive

When I was a kid the Green Cross Code was a big deal in school and on the TV. 'Stop, Look, Listen' was the instruction to live by. This would keep us all safe when crossing the road. Nowadays it's slightly longer.

*Think

*Stop

*Look & Listen

*Wait

*Look & Listen again

*Arrive Alive

I reckon we could all do with a little Green Cross Code in our lives when it comes to learning from the best. Think about who truly inspires you. Make time to really focus on what they do and why. Really pay attention to the detail. Take it in. Repeat. And when you're feeling inspired and energized, go smash it your way. Alive.

9. Good Things Really Do Come to an End

'Waking up to who you are requires letting go of who you imagine yourself to be.'

—Alan Watts

Not all of them. But many do. Sometimes it's a nice natural end and sometimes it all comes crashing down. When we're fully immersed in it we never anticipate the crash. Friendships, marriages, careers, fitness, dreams, winning, our favourite people and even you. Often it can hurt but at the same time it can often be for the best. It might not feel like it in the moment but there's always a reason. And of course, it's what we then do about it that really matters. If it requires a day of lying in bed stuffing ice cream in your face while feeling sorry for yourself then do it. But don't do it for too long because the fucking ice cream will come to an end. Be sad, be angry, be offline, be whatever you want to be. And then fill your head back up with goodness. Your heart will follow. Remember, it's all in the thinking.

10. Silliness Is Good for the Soul

I'm not entirely sure there is such a thing as a work–life balance. You wake up in the morning and you go to sleep at night. Everything in between is life. In saying that, slogging away for hours on end, continuously adding to your 'to-do' list, burning yourself out just to pay the bills isn't good for anyone.

Life can get serious. Finding reasons to laugh, lighten up and welcome some nonsense into your day is not only important, it's damn good for you. There is a whole science behind silliness but there is no science to actually being silly. Show Serious the door and welcome her distant cousin Silly in with open arms.

Research shows us that adults only laugh on average 17 times per day. That's 1.4 laughs an hour. There is an old school, urban legend that tells us children laugh 300–400 times per day. Now, who am I to diss this but all I'm saying is that if it's true then based on being awake for 12 hours children would be laughing at least once every 1–2 minutes from sunrise till sunset. True or not, it's fair to say, however, that kids definitely laugh more than us.

True story…

> Kian (aged 3): Daddy would you like to meet my new train?
>
> Me: I'd love to!
>
> Kian: I've given him a new name.
>
> Me: Cool, what's he called?
>
> Kian: Fucker. Fucker the Train
>
> Me: Kian where did you learn that word?
>
> Kian: What word?
>
> Me: The new name…
>
> Kian: I just made it up, I like it. Fucker.
>
> Me: I like Oliver. Let's go with Oliver.

I still see the silly in this conversation. Totally innocent and very, very funny.

11. Regrets, I've Had a Few…

If only…

What if…?

Forgive yourself for all the things you didn't do. Sounds easy but we all know it's incredibly difficult to do. Regret hurts every day. I used to spend months living in the past, feeling sorry for myself. Then someone introduced me to 're-do's'.

Choose the past memory that's hurting you the most. Imagine you could go back and do it all again. Write down how you would have done things differently and in doing so, allow yourself to pick out and embrace all the key learning points. This allows us to affirm that we have learned a lot more from our past mistake than we realized, and that if we had the skills we have now, back then, we would have done things differently.

Now I ask myself, 'What if I had never even tried?'. This is followed by so many positive, beautiful answers. So much so that I can look back with nothing but love.

Everything in life is impermanent. We must remember to appreciate everyone and everything in the moment, at every stage.

12. No One Really Knows What They're Doing

We're all just winging it, right? Making it all up as we go.

I am.

I find something that works, I do it more. I find something that doesn't, I don't do it again. Something feels right, I do it. It doesn't feel right, I don't do it.

I guess there's an element of trusting our gut instinct. Taking risks. Our bodies tell us when we're in danger but they also tell us when we're on to something.

Don't compare yourself to others, be inspired by them instead because it's highly likely they, too, are just ad-libbing at life!

13. Grudge Match

This is a hard one for me. I have spent years holding grudges. I am not the best at forgiving but I am getting so much better. It took me a long time to appreciate that I am owed nothing and I can literally feel the weight coming off my shoulders the more I choose to forgive.

As Confucius said, 'To be wronged is nothing, unless you continue to remember it.'

'Stop trying to make everyone happy, you're not Africa by Toto.'

—Anon

14. Be the Milk

You know when you pour cereal into a bowl without checking first to see if you have milk…and you don't have milk?

Basically, life is like a big bowl of Rice Krispies. Childhood, school, exams, interviews, jobs, hobbies, relationships, everything is just one great big giant bowl of Rice Krispies.

Imagine an empty bowl and you fill it with Rice Krispies. Just Rice Krispies, no milk yet, please don't get ahead of me here. Just Rice Krispies on their own, nothing else.

How would you describe them?

Plain. Still. Muted. Pale. Crispy. Dull. Dry. Bland. Parched. Basic. Thirsty. Dusty. Boring. Uneventful. Beige. They are simply not exciting. They are lifeless until you add the magic ingredient…

The milk.

Then what happens?

They come alive. They rise. They Snap, Crackle and Pop…they fizz, they bang, they whizz. They float! You can see them moving in the bowl in front of you, some even fall over the side.

Captivating, pleasing, enticing, magical, absorbing, mesmerizing, alluring, lively, uplifting…I'm sure you get my point.

You add the milk and shit gets exciting.

And if we don't get stuck in quickly, devour the Rice Krispies, top them up, refresh them and whack some sugar on from time to time then what happens?

They turn to mush, they become soggy. You don't want them and guess what, neither does anyone else.

So if life is the Rice Krispies then that must make us…the milk!

And if we don't get stuck into school, our jobs, our life, then fairly quickly what's going to happen? It's going to turn to mush, it's going to become a bit soggy. Might even turn sour.

We need to devour life, top it up when needed, refresh it when needed and whack some sugar on when you have to because, let's be honest, sometimes we need to sugar-coat things. Just remember you're not Willy Wonka but still, occasionally shit needs to be sweetened.

So, to finish this chapter with a sentence I've never used to finish a chapter before...

Be the milk.

CHAPTER 4

Live Deliberately

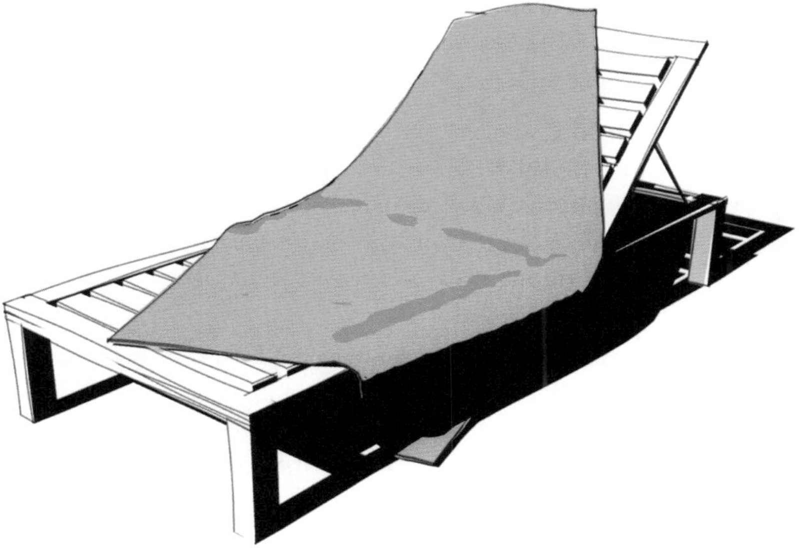

In life, there are those who do and those who don't. How we use our time, energy and effort is ultimately a choice. Wherever you're at, whatever you're doing, you can either give it your all or you can give it less. It's simple, there's no in-between, you're either giving it everything or you're not giving it everything.

It's easy to think about this in work or sporting terms but what about our thinking? Are you actively giving your thinking some thought? Are you thinking about your thinking?

The brain is really rather malleable. It's amazing what happens when you give your thought some thought...

The Sun Lounger Principle (SLP)

We've all heard of NLP, or neuro-linguistic programming, right? Described by Richard Bandler (founder) as 'an attitude of curiosity and a willingness to experiment that has left behind a trail of techniques'. One of my favourites is that NLP is essentially an 'instruction or owner's manual for the mind'. *Science Digest* describes it as 'the most powerful vehicle for change in existence'.

Now, I'm not prepared to argue with anyone on NLP and its benefits; I love (some of) it and while I believe it offers so much to so many, I think it has also got a tad crowded in its offerings. NLP practitioners are now in abundance and among the greats, unfortunately, we now have the ones who are kinda making shit up. I'll leave that there for now.

This is SLP. The Sun Lounger Principle.

The Sun Lounger Principle is a simple technique that anyone can apply to their thinking. It's most commonly used by dickheads on holiday but it can be used as a force for good.

So what is The Sun Lounger Principle? In its simplest form, SLP (Like NLP in many ways, just a bit easier to get your head around) is all in our thinking. It is a technique that enables you to quickly get to grips with a task you perhaps otherwise can't be bothered doing.

BUT with energy, enthusiasm, vigour and a great big 'I'M A FUCKING NINJA AT THIS' attitude.

It could be pinging out of bed on a Monday morning, tidying the house, cooking, going to the gym or even studying.

So how does it work?

Simple.

You treat every single day as if it were one big phat (that's fat with a PH) marvellous summer vacation.

'Surely that can't be right?' I hear you say…

OK, well let's imagine a regular, more normal, everyday type of start to the day.

Picture the scenario…

Alarm is set early. Let's imagine it's a gym day. Earlier than normal. Earlier than anyone else. Why? Because you're going to be first. You're going to be the best. The plan is to get up on the first alarm and move fast. You've done your prep. Everything you need is packed and ready. As you close your eyes it's all you can think about, it's hugely important, it's a make or break scenario. Prepared and motivated like never before, you fall asleep.

The alarm sounds. You shit yourself. It's awful, you snooze your alarm. You continue to snooze your alarm five more times. Your self-belief is almost non-existent. You're 20 minutes past your planned time of rising, you have to drag yourself out of bed. You feel sick and for a few minutes you allow yourself to reconsider. 'I could just do it tomorrow.' And just as you are about to go back to sleep you grab your stuff and you're gone.

You arrive at your destination; a few like-minded people have the same idea. You're frustrated that you weren't there earlier but, in your mind, these other people are not like you. They're better than you. They demotivate you instantly, 'I'll never be able to what they do' crosses your mind.

You've done it though. You got there even if you didn't quite give it your all. Your commitment is entirely questionable. You made a plan, almost stuck to it and barely saw it through to the end. You *kind* of made it happen and you feel guilty. You could've done so much better. There's no sense of pride, zero smugness.

And you know deep down that you'll probably do this every single day, even when you know that in this particular moment of your life, there's nothing more important. You've entirely half-assed the whole thing.

These moments rarely inspire us.

OK, let's get back to those big phat summery days.

Think about a time you spent an absolute fortune to get away for two weeks' chill-out in the sun. You'd been dreaming about it for 12 months. You could almost taste it the closer it got. Sunshine, me time, beautiful food and drink, pure magic. Bliss.

You arrive.

You dump your bags in your room and decide to have nosey around, you know, get your bearings.

You're scoping the joint.

But for what?

Prime sun lounger spot. That's what. Some people this comes more naturally to than others. It's practically subconscious. Stealth-like.

Some of us need to work at it much harder. Like all ninja-related activity, there are levels.

I mean there's stuff to think about. Space, shade, direction, chavs, bar, pool, noise, water polo, the other chavs and how far are you from your room.

It's now late and you're slowly losing the feeling that we all have when we first arrive somewhere new. The 'Hmm not sure about this place yet, last year was better' feeling.

Bedtime.

Alarm set.

6 a.m.

6 a.m.?

This is a holiday. You need no alarms. You're 'off'. Your brain is off. There's NOTHING TO DO. NOTHING NEEDS DOING.

But we all know this is untrue. There's a mission afoot.

And it's life or fucking death.

Sleep....

ALARM ALARM ALARM – it's 6 a.m.

You leap out of bed. You don't even touch the bed because that's how ninjas respond. You grab your towels and leave. You don't even open the door; you simply slip under it like a piece of A4 paper.

You glide down the corridors.

You meet a fellow ninja.

Like motorcyclists you nod to each other, there's mutual 6 a.m. respect but in your mind you're thinking 'You better not have your eye on my fucking spot dickhead', because it's yours right? You own it, right?

In this moment you own the entire fucking hotel.

Your walk becomes a mild jog. It's 6 a.m. on your £7000 holiday and you're jogging! But you're wearing flip-flops and that in itself requires real concentration, real effort and tremendous skill.

You see other joggers. You pick up the pace.

It. Is. On.

You feel your heart race, the blood is pumping.

Right now, in this moment in your life, you give the biggest fuck you've ever given.

You'll do whatever it takes.

ANYTHING.

You see your sun loungers.

They have no towels on them.

They're yours.

Time seems to slow down in the moment.

THIS FUCKING MATTERS.

And this is what I'm talking about my friend. This feeling right here that I'm describing.

This level of passion. This level of energy. This level of hunger.

This is The Sun Lounger Principle.

Take it and apply it to shit in your life that matters.

Your health. Your family. Your career. Your ability to help others.

And where does it all begin?

Just like NLP, in our heads.

This is the Sun Lounger Principle, let's apply it to our thinking.

'The cure for boredom is curiosity. There is no cure for curiosity.'

—Ellen Parr

A Curious Climate

I watched an interview with comedian and actor Eddie Izzard recently. In it he talked about how he believes that in life 'We've either got to be brave and curious or fearful and suspicious.' He was talking about his extraordinary achievements, his beliefs and his general outlook on life. He went on to confirm that in all he does he is always 'trying to be brave and curious'.

Brave and curious, I love this attitude to life, to thinking.

It's incredibly easy to *not* be brave and curious. If it was the other way round everyone would be doing it. I definitely find 'fearful and suspicious' much easier but let's be honest, it's not nearly as fun, is it? Or rewarding.

If we could ask every single person in the world if they would rather be brave and curious or fearful and suspicious, I think we know what the answer's going to be. And yet fearful and suspicious rules the heads of so many around the world.

But to be brave and curious is not to live without fear and suspicion. It's to suck the fear right up and do it anyway, even *in* moments of fear. Some of the bravest people I know are living day to day with anxiety on a level many will never know.

I urge you to get brave and curious about your thinking; it doesn't need to be complicated.

When I began my university career....

brief interlude

During 1997–2001 I completed an honours degree in Primary School Teaching. Yup, you read that correctly, I'm a fully qualified primary school teacher. Teaching is one of the greatest, most underrated professions in the world. To all the teachers out there, I love you. You are remarkable and deserve more resource, support, respect, money and holidays. Well, most of you. To the ones who are massive assholes who don't actually like kids, use fear and anger as your tools and have become a version of you that you said you'd never become, then you, you can fuck off because we don't need you in our classrooms.

normal service continues

When my university career began, right at the start we were introduced to the work of Dr Susan Greenfield. Like all successful scientists, writers, speakers and broadcasters, there are definitely two camps: the fans and the non-fans. Dr Greenfield can definitely split opinion but, hey, I'm not a psychologist, I'm not a scientist, nor have I ever claimed to be either of these things but if you like the sound of something, you try it and if it works for you then I think that's OK. Like yoga, mindfulness and NLP. If it works for you then what's the problem? I had never been introduced to anything like this before. I was learning some really cool stuff about the human brain and the power of our thinking. Through her teachings I was introduced to the likes of Freud, among others. I had never been taught this stuff before. I appreciate that psychology is commonplace in schools nowadays, but this shit was blowing my 18-year-old mind. This led me to my interest in psychology, and over time, more recently, positive psychology.

On the off-chance you've never heard of positive psychology, it is, in its essence, the scientific study of what makes life worth living. A science of positive aspects of human life, such as happiness, well-being and flourishing.

I'm sure you share with me its positive appeal.

Martin Seligman is recognized as the founder of positive psychology. In his words it can be summarized as a 'scientific study of optimal human functioning that aims to discover and promote the factors that allow individuals and communities to thrive'.

Count me in!

Basically, for most of its life mainstream psychology has been concerned with negative aspects of human life. This was not originally meant to be the case. The first psychologists had three main aims to their work, which was to:

1. Cure mental illness
2. Improve normal lives
3. Identify and nurture high talent

However, as you can imagine, World War 2 left a toxic legacy of ill health and depression. One of the most transformative events in history, conditions were extreme and humanity was staring an almighty crisis in the face. There were huge consequences and understandably points 2 and 3 pretty much got forgotten about. Of course, great results have come from the work, with depression, personality disorder and anxiety all now treatable.

So positive psychology is still just psychology, it just asks different questions, for example 'What is right with this person?' rather than 'What is wrong?' Much like what Eddie Izzard was saying, it's just a different way of seeing things. Of thinking things.

For the past 15 years I've worked incredibly hard to shift my thinking. My goal has been very much to move away from fear and suspicion and to embrace brave and curious. I've had some great results. Positive thinking has indeed affected my life in the most wonderful of ways. But I'm not perfect and I've slipped on many occasions. I have to work incredibly hard to get it right, and just like The Sun Lounger Principle, it takes real effort and energy.

It's often just small changes.

One of the most profound statements I ever read is that 'thoughts become things'. I'm not sure who said it first or where I got it from, but it's credited to Bob Proctor in his 1984 book *You Were Born Rich* and I am definitely a subscriber to this way of thinking.

Thoughts become things. Just to be clear, I don't mean that if you imagine a million pounds sitting in front of you that it will magically appear. I see it more as an 'if you turn up to work every day thinking it's going to be shit then it will be' kind of way.

Let's try something…

Opportunityisnowhere – what do you see?

It's highly likely that most of you read 'Opportunity is nowhere' and then went back and read it as 'Opportunity is now here'. Whilst this is just a play on words, so often in life we see, hear, feel the negative first. The key is to change it though. To allow our thinking to shift.

If you read it as 'Opportunity I snow here' then you're my favourite.

You'll meet super positive people all the time in life, the ones who appear to have it all sussed. It's not that they don't feel fear or things such as anxiety, it's that they choose to think about it in different ways. Bear in mind we need anxiety in our lives. It helps to keep us alive!

'Being positive doesn't mean you don't have negative thoughts. It just means you don't let those thoughts control your life.'

—Jay Shetty

In your workplace, for example, you'll have three camps of people. The positive thinkers, the negative thinkers and the in-betweeners who jump back and forth. I do occasionally find myself an in-betweener. I catch myself and make that conscious effort to turn it around.

Think about every place you've ever worked and now picture the staffroom on a Monday morning. Firstly, you'll have those who turn up like Mary Poppins with rays of light beaming out of their fucking face. They're my favourite. Practically perfect in every way. A joy. A delight. They remind you every day why you do what you do. It's infectious but not all appreciate their positivity.

Secondly, you'll have those who turn up like Mr Banks* with rays of lacklustre broadcasting out of their entire body. They're not my favourite. Practically frowning in every way. A trial. A tribulation. They remind you every day why you don't hang out with them. Unfortunately, whilst many don't appreciate their negativity, it can also be infectious.

Note Mr Banks turns out to be a super nice dude who cares deeply about people but over time he just needed to shift his thinking. Funny that. *Saving Mr Banks* is one of the most underrated movies of all time – get it watched!

Thirdly, those who do both brilliantly, depending on who they are talking to. Proper wannabes. The fakes. If there's anything this world doesn't need it's another fake fuck.

> ***Unfuckwithable***
> *adjective*
> when you're truly at peace and in touch with yourself, and nothing anyone says or does bothers you, and no negativity or drama can touch you.

Our mind is incredible, should we choose to use it. Sometimes a subtle change in our thinking can create a ripple strong enough to change our day for the better, to strengthen our relationships or to simply make us feel a little happier, a little more relaxed in our rush hour world.

Over time, however, it can change our lives.

No shit.

Ice Ice Baby

We've all seen those stunning split pictures of icebergs from both above and below the water. No matter how often I see them I'm always in awe of the sheer magnitude of the iceberg, especially the section below the water. This massive section of the iceberg is always around 90% of the full berg with the part that's visible above the water only ever around 10%.

Imagine your mind being like an iceberg. Neuroscientists at esteemed institutions like Stanford, Harvard, MIT and others have determined that the human brain operates in much the same way. Of all your thinking, 10% is conscious and a massive 90% is taken up by your subconscious and unconscious thinking.

So, what's the difference between subconscious and unconscious mind? In proper simple terms – a language I understand – the subconscious mind oversees our recent memories and is in non-stop contact with the resources of the unconscious mind.

Think of your unconscious mind as a giant warehouse that stores all your memories and past experiences. This includes everything that's no longer important to you, the stuff you've consciously forgotten about and all the shit that's been repressed though trauma. It's from these memories and experiences that our beliefs, habits, and behaviours are formed.

You with me?

Basically, your unconscious never stops chatting with your conscious mind. All their dealings go through your subconscious and this is what provides you with the meaning to all your interactions with the world, as filtered through your beliefs and habits. It communicates through feelings, emotions, imagination, sensations, and dreams.

Aye?

It takes a great big massive event or a nice wee technique to unlock the memories in your unconscious, unlike the subconscious where we can choose to remember.

Imagine it as thoughts being closer to the surface. If I ask you now to tell me your phone number you'd be able to tell me even though prior to me asking you had no conscious thought about your phone number. This information is closer to the surface and with a little focus you can remember it.

But here's the cool part: you can use this to change your life. That's a pretty massive claim but it's absolutely true and all you have to do is subtly change the way you think. That's it! But it all starts in the conscious mind, the easiest part to control. After all, this is exactly how your habits and behaviours were formed in the first place.

I've made the shift from being an incredibly negative person to a much more positive, happier individual. I've still got work to do and, as mentioned earlier, I sometimes find myself running programs in my head that I thought were long gone, but fuck me it's worth the effort to up my game.

The mindset we choose for ourselves is just that, a choice. Choice lives in your conscious mind but if you've spent your whole life so far choosing to hate Mondays then guess what, dear reader, it's no longer conscious, it's well and truly in there. It's in you. Dr Andy Cope reminds us that Mondays are a seventh of our life and I'm pretty certain there are individuals out there who spend a seventh of their life less happy simply because it's a fucking Monday.

I recently put this to the test with a unique little experiment. I stood outside Waverley train station early one dreich Monday morning in Edinburgh with an enormous bunch of balloons, each one bright and beautiful. Helium of course.

What made this slightly different from any old Monday was that this was Blue Monday, officially recognized as the most depressing day of the year. Of course, it's all bollocks and was invented as part of a marketing campaign to encourage us to part with our hard earned cash and book summer holidays. But hey, we humans fucking embraced it, and now it's a thing. Again, FFS.

So, instead of Blue Monday, we went with Balloon Monday.

I met commuters as they piled off their trains and began to hand out the balloons.

'Have a great start to the week!' I said, holding out a balloon for them to take. It very quickly became clear that I was the odd one out. The weirdo, the freak.

'Why would you do such a thing?' asked one suited gentleman.

'Why would you not?' I replied.

'On a Monday morning? You must be mental!' he said.

Or maybe I just want to help kick other people's weeks off with a splash of colour? Why save it just for the weekend?

You'll be glad to hear that as time passed, I began to meet like-minded individuals who appreciated their gift of a balloon. Smiles appeared. Faces lit up. (You can see the whole thing on YouTube.)

'Nobody can be uncheered with a balloon.'

—A.A. Milne

For generations we've practised and practised our lack of love for the humble Monday. Now it's a thing and it's in us good and proper.

What if we consciously tried to reverse it?

What if we consciously decide to love a Monday as much as a Friday?

But just how does one 'Friday their Monday'?

Easy, change your thinking.

Friday Your Monday

Think about how you learned to ride a bike. In my day we hadn't thought of the genius that is balance bikes. We had good old stabilizers and when it was time for them to come off my old man held the back of my seat, ran alongside me and when he thought the time was right, he let go. I think it's fair to say the time wasn't always right.

Sometimes he'd just take off one, but I'd just go round in circles. I'm sure there's a metaphor somewhere in this.

But that's how I learned to ride my bike. Consciously thinking 'left leg, right leg, brake, steer, balance' over and over again until I no longer had to. Now I don't think about it and I haven't had to since I was about four. It's now subconscious. Just like swimming, driving, cooking, brushing my teeth and many many other things. Over time they all became a thing, they're in me.

All the examples I've given you above are physical actions and movements. So how does it work with our thinking? The same.

Imagine you were walking through your house carrying a glass of juice and someone said to you 'Don't spill that!' – what's the first thing you picture clearly in your conscious mind?

Exactly! You spilling the juice…and then what happens? Right again, you spill it. It's ridiculous, they tell you not to spill your juice so then you basically pour it all over your own head.

It reminds me of the time my wife and I moved into our first house and we had to replace all the carpets. I had no idea that Ali would create a list of rules for said carpets. This was pre-kids, obviously! In the living room for example; no eating, no drinking and no shoes! NOTHING touches the carpet. You had to float.

I came in from work one evening. Shoes off, I hovered across the carpet to the sofa…that's a skill. As I sat down I noticed a cup of tea on the floor. I don't drink tea so it clearly wasn't mine. Ali was coming down the stairs and I couldn't contain my excitement at the fact that Ali had broken her own rule! For once it wasn't me getting it wrong.

She entered the room, this was my moment. I could barely contain myself.

'Ali, there's a cup of tea here on the new carpet…'

Ali replied, 'It's mine,' picked up her tea and carried on drinking it.

After a few minutes, I realized that was the end of the conversation.

Another few minutes passed and I plucked up some courage…

'But you said we weren't allowed to eat or drink in the living room.'

Placing the tea down again, she said 'No…*you're* not allowed! So, whatever you do, don't knock my tea onto the new carpet….'

You see, I heard what she said, I do listen. But my leg, it was already moving. And it moved in a way that it's never moved before. I put the most beautiful spin on the cup and I learned just how far tea can travel!

In her best teacher's voice she roared at me,

'I told you not to do that!'

I think that's why I did it. By Ali telling me not to do something, an image popped into my conscious mind and BOOM, it happened. So, in a kind of roundabout way, this was Ali's fault…

So I said,

'Ali, in a weird kind of way, this was your fault…'

Anyone?

'Maybe you should clean up the tea…?' I continued.

I cleaned up the tea.

With my face.

But us humans are incredible, right? We just need to think things and they happen. Remember when you were in school and running along the corridor? A teacher would shout 'DON'T RUN!' and you'd be gone in a puff of smoke. It's funny how the word 'Don't' can make us 'Do'. But if the teacher calmly said, 'walk', we'd walk.

Thoughts become things.

The more you think about something, the more it becomes real.

We're born with zero religious beliefs. And yet…

'"Of course there must be lots of magic in the world" he said wisely one day, "but people don't know what it is like or how to make it. Perhaps the beginning is just to say nice things are going to happen until you make them happen, I am going to try and experiment."'

—Frances Hodgson Burnett, The Secret Garden

We tell people every single day how we feel about ourselves. Think about how many times per day someone asks, 'How are you?', 'How's things?', 'How you doing?', 'How you feeling?' and so on. There must be days we need to answer that question dozens of times, maybe hundreds depending on your job!

I often wonder what these questions actually mean. Like, I know literally what they mean but does the other person truly want to know how I am and, if so, how long an answer is appropriate? It's very rare to stop and offer a full thesis on just how our day is panning out or how successful our evening was last night. For this very reason we are often guilty of giving short, perhaps even one-word answers.

'Fine', 'OK' and 'Not bad' are popular responses. Sometimes they might be followed with a 'thanks'. Occasionally we might hear a 'Good' or if we're really lucky perhaps a 'Wonderful', but these are few and far between.

Then there are those who just give it to you…

'Shite.'

One of my favourites is 'Don't get me started'… AND THEN THEY FUCKING START!

'Fine' is the number one response. But just what does it mean? Is it good, is it bad, is it neither? Is it somewhere in the middle? Is it Average? Is it 'Meh'?

The 'Meh Brigade' definitely exist in workplaces the world over. There's no translation needed anywhere, it's the same word in every country. A wee shrug of the shoulders, a slight hand gesture and 'Meh' tells us exactly how someone is feeling.

If you go to a fine dining restaurant, aside from tiny portions and a huge bill, what do you expect? The best meal of your life, right? Fine art? Worth millions. Fine silks? Expensive lingerie. Fine wine? Extraordinary body and flavour. Tesco Finest? OK, maybe not that one…

Fine

adjective, fin·er, fin·est.

1. of superior or best quality. Exceptional; of high or highest grade: *fine wine.*
2. choice, excellent, or admirable: *a fine painting.*

If someone asks you how you are and you tell them you are 'fine', are we telling them we are exceptional? Probably not. Most are probably using 'fine' as a simple tool to bypass the other person and not get into much of a conversation. Fine has lost its true meaning. Somehow, it's shifted from 'exceptional' to 'meh'.

It's happened over time, it's become a thing. It's in us.

But let's go back to the iceberg and learning to ride a bike, let's think about this for a moment. What if you're 'fine' 20 times a day? What if you consciously, out loud, state many many times a day that you are fine? And yet you believe 'fine' means 'meh'…do we begin to feel 'meh'?

Meh

exclamation

expressing a lack of interest or enthusiasm. 'meh, I'm not impressed so far'

adjective

uninspiring; unexceptional. 'a lot of his movies are … meh'

Maybe it's time to redefine fine and claim it back!

What if our response is always 'busy' or 'fair to middling' or 'bored' or 'tired' or 'stressed'?

Is it possible that over time they become a thing, in us?

One of the best responses I've heard is 'I've heard various opinions, what's yours?'

What if we flipped our thinking on this and made a conscious effort to answer in a much more positive way? Is it possible that over time we essentially write ourselves a new program? I know people who don't believe in the whole positive thinking/language thing but 15 years ago I was curious enough to give it a go.

Try it. I dare you. Give it time and see what happens. Notice how you feel and pay attention to how others around you change with you. This is so simple and so obvious it's borderline patronizing.

But seriously, if there's one thing I've learned about this shit, it's this:

If you want to live and work in a beautiful world that is kind, loving and awesome then you need to take some accountability for the energy you put out.

Do it on purpose. Do it *with* purpose. In other words, live deliberately.

Stick with it, you'll begin to feel different. And when you get stuck at the water fountain chatting with the 'Meh Brigade' at work, keep doing it.

I dare you to go all-out-batshit-crazy-positive with 'Bloody fabulous' or 'Utterly tremendous'!

Truth is though, you're going to get weird looks and your colleagues will probably begin to avoid you. Might not be a bad thing…

In all seriousness though, how hard is it to reply with 'Good thanks, how are you?' and fucking mean it?

Look, it's a start. Remember, this is about getting curious with our thinking, it's about being brave with our language. Who knows, it might lead to:

- The total package.
- I'M MARY POPPINS Y'ALL!
- Straight-up godly.
- Pushing 11.
- Dancing to the rhythm of life.
- Happy and you know it. [*clap your hands*]

OK, maybe I'm taking the piss now but, just for fun, if you really want to be a total dick you could just go with:

- Like you, but better.
- If I were doing any better, I'd hire you to enjoy it with me.
- Doing well, unless you have intentions of ruining my day with your face.
- Horrible, now that I've met you.

Every single minute of every single day, your body is physically reacting, literally changing, in response to the thoughts that run through your mind. The way you think about yourself is serious.

'Watch your thoughts; They become words. Watch your words; They become actions. Watch your actions; They become habits. Watch your habits; They become character. Watch your character; It becomes your destiny.'

—Unknown

There's actual science at play here. Crazy psychology shit that people have been writing about for years and yet we still have work places up and down the country full of miserable fuckers moaning about EVERYTHING.

Writer and brain injury survivor Debbie Hampton reminds us that 'For years research has proved that just thinking about something can cause your brain to release neurotransmitters, chemical messengers that allow it to communicate with parts of itself and your nervous system. Neurotransmitters control virtually all of your body's functions, from hormones to digestion to feeling happy, sad, or stressed.'

The power of thought is extraordinary. Research shows us time and time again that when we move our thinking from negative to positive, from fearful and suspicious to brave and curious we feel physically and mentally better for it, resulting in real outcomes, such as having more energy and reduced anxiety.

In *The Intention Experiment: Using Your Thoughts to Change Your Life and the World*, Lynne McTaggart writes:

'A sizable body of research exploring the nature of consciousness, carried on for more than thirty years in prestigious scientific institutions around the world, shows that thoughts are capable of affecting everything from the simplest machines to the most complex living beings. This evidence suggests that human thoughts and intentions are an actual physical "something" with astonishing power to change our world. Every thought we have is tangible energy with the power to transform. A thought is not only a thing; a thought is a thing that influences other things.'

A thought is an electrochemical event taking place in your nerve cells producing a cascade of physiological changes. Jordan Lejuwaan explains it this way:

'There are thousands upon thousands of receptors on each cell in our body. Each receptor is specific to one peptide, or protein. When we have feelings of anger, sadness, guilt, excitement, happiness or nervousness, each separate emotion releases its own flurry of neuropeptides. Those peptides surge through the body and connect with those receptors which change the structure of each cell as a whole. Where this gets interesting is when the cells actually divide. If a cell has been exposed to a certain peptide more than others, the new cell that is produced through its division will have more of the receptor that matches with that specific peptide. Likewise, the cell will also have less receptors for peptides that its mother/sister cell was not exposed to as often.'

So, if you have been hammering your cells with peptides from negative thoughts, you are literally programming your cells to receive more of the same negative peptides in the future. What's even worse is that you're lessening the number of receptors of positive peptides on the cells, making yourself more inclined towards negativity.

Unfuck Yourself

Be who you were before all that stuff happened that dimmed your fucking shine.

Every cell in your body is replaced about every two months. So, the good news is, you can reprogram your pessimistic cells to be more optimistic by adopting positive thinking practices, like *mindfulness* and *gratitude*, for permanent results.

'A pessimist sees the difficulty in every opportunity; an optimist sees the opportunity in every difficulty.'

—Winston Churchill

'How are you?' is such a simple, everyday kind of question that we just pass off as meaningless chit-chat. But not only is it an excellent way to start a conversation with others, it's a fantastic opportunity to express your optimism and share it with others. Being optimistic can be fairly simple but remaining optimistic can be difficult, exhausting at times.

But is it worth it?

This is fairly easy to answer. I'm pretty sure you know the answer but read any of the research out there and you'll discover an extraordinary number of selfish reasons to be choose optimism over pessimism.

Here's just a few to blow your mind…

- Optimism has been proven to improve the immune system, prevent chronic disease and help people cope with unfortunate news.
- Pessimistic people tend to view problems as internal, unchangeable and pervasive, whereas optimistic people are the opposite.
- Pessimism has been linked with depression, stress, and anxiety whereas optimism has been shown to serve as a protective factor against depression,

as well as several serious medical problems, including coronary heart disease.
- Optimism is linked to life longevity. Optimism also plays a role in the recovery from illness and disease.
- Optimists are also able to recover from disappointments more quickly.
- Optimists are also more likely to engage in problem solving when faced with difficulties, which is itself associated with increased psychological well-being.

As you can see there is a common theme here: realistic optimism can have profound effects on a person's physical health.

It's clear that optimism is a force for good and will help to keep us healthy, happy and alive. This news is great for people who are 'natural' optimists, but what about others who don't generally 'look on the bright side'? Can 'natural' pessimists learn to become more optimistic?

Yes. And I'm the perfect example. I think being a pessimist is a little like being an addict, in the way of once a pessimist, always a pessimist. I just need to work that bit harder to stay off the pessimism. If I fall off the wagon and allow my pessimism to start again then it can lead to a real setback, the floodgates open and there's a knock-on impact on all those around me.

Whilst there are still huge amounts of research to be done in this area it would appear that optimism can be learned. Whilst not entirely conclusive, some studies suggest that optimism lies – at least in part – in our genes. I would have guessed this. My dad was the pessimist's pessimist, a legend in his own pessimism. It's well and truly in my genes.

But I have – for the most part – turned this around. And it all began when I simply changed my thinking.

I read a book called *Tuesdays With Morrie* about 15 years ago. It's written by Mitch Albom. The book focuses on the relationship of the author with his teacher, whose words turn his life around 20 years after losing touch. While there are many lessons to be learned from Morrie – a few of which are peppered throughout this book – there was one key moment for me.

And it's this…

Morrie: *'Part of the problem is that everyone is in such a hurry. People haven't found meaning in their lives, so they're running all the time looking for it. They think the next car, the next house, the next job. Then they find those things are empty, too, and they keep running.'*

Mitch: *'Once you start running, it's hard to slow yourself down.'*

This was me. Jumping from one thing to the next. Idea after idea, on the road to 'making it', always fearing that if I stopped, I'd miss my chance.

Everyone is in such a hurry that we're not seeing what's in front of us right here, right now. And if we're constantly running and pushing for what's next then it's very hard to be optimistic.

Sometimes it's still me. I catch myself and have to make a conscious effort to be grateful for all that I have in my life. My family, my health, a home, a job that I love, friends… the list goes on. Yes, there's a lot I still want to achieve in my career but the hurry needs to slow, the constant chase needs to slow.

None of this 'Be a shark', 'Be a wolf' shite. I much prefer to be a kind, humble human that appreciates the magic in all they have and all those around them.

This doesn't come naturally to me but what I've learned is that happiness isn't found in things; it's gratitude for what we have that creates happiness.

Thanks to the world of positive psychology, it has become clear that there are several advantages associated with being grateful. Among other things, grateful people are happier, have stronger feelings of social support, have better physical health, increased empathy and feel less stressed and depressed. Being grateful has so many positive attributes. I have found that working hard to increase my levels of gratitude has increased my feelings of well-being. And I find the more I express gratitude the better I sleep. I simply feel stronger.

Gratitude journaling is a well-known positive psychology intervention and regardless of who you are, or the circumstances of your life, the health benefits of gratitude are undeniable. There are numerous gratitude books, workbooks, apps, and pre-made journals available, making it easier for us all to get it right.

Some people journal every day, others a couple of times a week. It's about working out what's right for you, as the benefits are really worth it!

I started out with 'Happy Stories in Three Words'. Literally writing a happy story about my day, every night before bed. But only in three words. This is a great way to begin, as it really forced me to focus in on what went right in my day, what made me happy and just what was important. It's also a lot more complicated than you might think. It became easier and easier as I went along and my three-word stories became 10 words which became 100 words until I found myself writing as much as felt right in that moment.

Sometimes I just write a list of things I'm grateful for. Or people. It doesn't have to be deep; it can be as simple as you want but remember it's for your eyes only so if you want to express yourself further then take it away!

Another wonderful gratitude exercise is to write a letter to someone you are incredibly grateful for. Pour everything out on to the page, thanking them for all they have done, really detailing why they mean so much to you and the difference they made in your life. You don't even have to send them the letter if you feel anxious about it, but I can assure you, there is nothing to feel anxious about. Not only will you feel a real kick from writing it, the lucky recipient will, too.

The next level of this is to pick up the phone and read it to them. Or better still read it to them in person, telling them to their actual face, with your face.

Rather than complain about all you don't have in your life and all that you feel is wrong with the world, let's make that shift in our thinking. Allow yourself time in your day to focus on all that you do have and all that is right in your world. It takes real practice, just like riding a bike. You might fall off a few times but the more you stick with it, the easier it gets until it's just the norm.

Until it's in you.

But we need to commit. Remember, if you take off just one stabilizer, you'll go round in circles.

Feed that conscious mind of yours. Optimism is healthy, let's infect our minds with this stuff and in turn maybe we can infect the world and inspire others to be more brave and curious and to live deliberately.

'You and I are not what we eat; we are what we think.'

—Walter Anderson

Not only will you sleep better, you'll live longer.

Thank you.

CHAPTER 5

The Real Feel

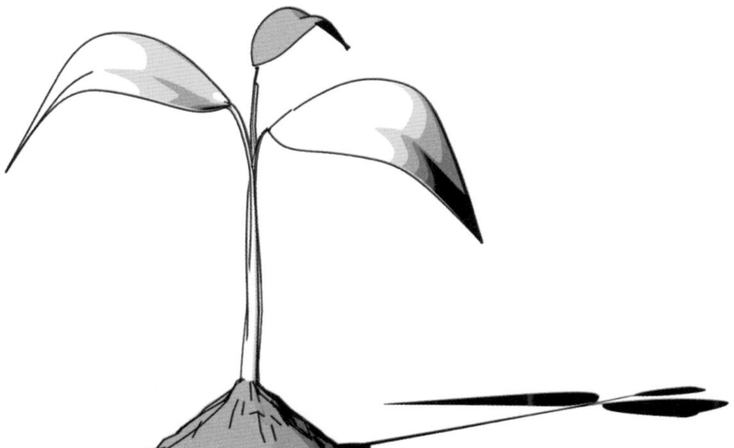

'Try to make at least one person happy every day, and then in ten years you may have made three thousand and fifty persons happy, or brightened a small town by your contribution to the fund of general enjoyment.'

—Sydney Smith

What the Fuck Is Happiness Anyway?

In 1977 – two years before I was born – representing the Wycliffe Missionary, Daniel Everett travelled to Amazonia to try and convert the Pirahã people to follow the way of the Bible. Instead, they converted him, he abandoned his faith, discovered new values and left his old life behind.

Why?

Simple, he found what he believed were the happiest people in the world. And he wanted some of what they were having.

It took Daniel a while to get to know and fully understand the tribe. Originally, he was seen as a threat and the men of the Pirahã had all sorts of plans to kill him. But with time he won them round, and what he discovered is truly fascinating and holds several of the keys to happiness.

The Pirahã are fascinating for a number of reasons. As Aleksandar Mishkov tells us, the main one is that their culture is based on immediate experience. The here and now.

Over the last few years how many personal development books have we all read highlighting this? Every. Single. One!

You just need to Google 'What is happiness?' and very quickly you'll be reading something about being present or in the moment.

Members of the primitive tribe are said to be the most simple and happiest people living on Mother Earth, basing their knowledge on facts and relationships. They have a pretty damn awesome way of living and the more I learn, the more I love their philosophies and the more I'm inspired by them.

Things Just Happen

First up, it's all about accepting things as they are.

There's no such thing as politeness within the Pirahã tribe. This might seem completely backward in relation to our culture but it makes sense to them. They believe politeness only shows a lack of trust in one another. Everything is/should be centred around love, support and understanding each other. The Pirahã tribe do not question or try to reason things too much.

Children are not punished or shouted at and the only explanation and reasoning they have is 'it just happened'.

And that's it.

It reminds me of me at the age of about 10, sitting on my bedroom floor surrounded by mess. Clothes, Lego, Transformers, everything everywhere and my mum telling me to get it tidied. My response was always 'But this is who I am, it's just how it is.' That didn't cut it for me, obviously.

It's far too easy to get weighed down with all that modern life expects of us, increasingly becoming more difficult to let shit go as we overthink everything. Earlier I referenced The Beatles' 'Let it Be' in the 1960s and then *Frozen*'s 'Let it Go' more recently, but it turns out the Pirahã had it nailed long before.

The Pirahã do not question things nor try to see 'deeper' aspects of feelings or situations. As a black belt in overthinking this appeals to me in so many ways! Natural occurrences are not questioned.

Things just happen.

If a rebellious teenager wants to be alone for the whole day or sit in their mess – fine, you are free to do anything you want as long as you are willing to not eat all day. This would be my downfall. Nae dinner? Not a chance.

Xibipíío

I referenced 'immediate experience' earlier. In the Pirahã tribe experiencing things means everything. Literally.

A client of mine once told me that the best advice he ever received was that '*to assume was to make a huge mistake*', his thinking being that if you're assuming stuff then you're making shit up. If you're assuming something, then you're not dealing in fact.

Everett discovered that the Pirahã culture is bothered only with matters that fall within their direct personal experience, and therefore there is no undefined past or future, only their current personal experience and living memory. *Xibipíío*, meaning 'experiential liminality', describes something 'experienceable' or experienced. They do not value past or future, but instead focus on now. The tribe does not understand unexperienced past; namely, unless you saw it, heard it or deduced it from other available evidence then Pirahã people will not believe you.

> *'Never let the future disturb you. You will meet it, if you have to, with the same weapons of reason which today arm you against the present.'*
>
> *—Marcus Aurelius*

So basically, there's no dwelling on the past, zero worrying about the future and bullshit isn't even a thing. No lies, no exaggeration, no making stuff up. There are no rumours, no falsities, no gossip, no hearsay. Can you imagine? Life would be a lot simpler without such bullshit.

Xibipíío ladies and gentlemen…experiencing, living in the present. Now.

You Are Responsible for Your Own Work

One of the strongest Pirahã values is that they don't believe in coercion; you simply don't tell other people what to do. You don't force, you don't command or even give advice, and everyone knows what they have to do without being told so. Since there is no social hierarchy, no one is 'better' or 'worse' than the other one. The tribe doesn't have leaders. Everyone is equal and everyone is equally good. Imagine this at work? Or better still, in modern day politics?

There is no hierarchy, no theft, no crime. They have no property or prejudice. They sing during the night and believe dreams and reality are equally important. They also happen to change their names every seven years, I like this, I might try it. The Pirahã have no knowledge of dates or calendars and within their culture there is no god and no myths.

From my readings it would appear that such tribes as Pirahã show that happiness lies in small, daily activities. The more we try to complicate, the worse our lives become. It seems it's quite easy to be happy, as long as you do not overcomplicate your life. Or your thinking.

'How simple it is to see that we can only be happy now, and there will never be a time when it is not now.'

—Gerald Jampolsky

We have celebrities nowadays that write books about this shit. The Guide to De-Cluttering, How to Tidy Your Fucking House, Get Rid of all Your Stuff, Live Slowly, The Art of Cosiness, Do Less and Be More, Think Less, Worry Less, Don't Give a Fuck. OK, you get the point.

I believe this is one of the biggest contributing factors to our unhappiness. We've overcomplicated everything. Our world got busy and in return our brains got busy. The modern world is getting busier and yes, folks, our brains are getting busier.

Where does it end?

I was recently introduced to a fantastic series of blogs by The School of Life. While everything I've read from them so far has been excellent, there is one stand-out for me: *How the Modern World Makes Us Mentally Ill.*

It reminds us that in many ways the modern world is, in fact, fantastic BUT, and it's a big BUT, it's also 'tragically geared to causing a high background level of anxiety and widespread low-level depression'.

So, is the modern world really making us ill and if so, how? Just what's stopping us from being happy? And calm? And present?

School of Life believes that the problems lie within Meritocracy, Individualism, Secularism, Romanticism, Media, Perfectibility. Let's explore these…

Meritocracy

Now I'm not going to lie, I didn't know what meritocracy even meant until recently. So if I can paraphrase, basically, our societies tell us that everyone is free to make it if they have the talent and energy. We have it drummed into us from a young age that if we're talented enough and we have the passion then we'll make it, we can be anything we ever dreamt of being. Where this falls down, however, is if we fail or don't quite fulfil our ambition, well, then we must be a bit shit, lacking in talent or just lazy. This creates a divided society where those deemed to be the best must then be deserving of all their success, leaving the rest of us to be worthy of our shitness. Not just unfortunate, but losers. When my comedy career came to an end – twice – this is exactly how I felt.

Again, striving to 'make it' causes a huge amount of grief for so many. We weren't shit, we had talent and we worked damned hard. But we didn't 'make it'. Or did we? We were happy. We were making other people happy. We were having fun and being creative. In hindsight, we totally made it. We made it big time. And yet as time went on, the more we were judged, the more the pressure grew, the more 'successful' we wanted to be, the less happy we became.

This applies to so many of us in our lives and careers. Doesn't matter what your job is. Nurse, full-time mum, joiner, teacher, whatever. The desire and or pressure to 'make it' for some simply doesn't end. But what are we chasing? Happiness? Fulfilment? Acknowledgement? Recognition?

Remember, happiness isn't a race. There's no chase. You *can* dictate the pace. I keep reading this back in Eminem's voice…

Individualism

I touched on individualism in Chapter 2, writing about my love of all things 'togetherness'. I shared my burning ambition to belong to a movement, a purpose that can be shared, creating, shaping, succeeding and sharing with others. I'm often asked why I've never gone out on my own in business or comedy. I genuinely love to be a part of something. It's simply not about me. We live in a time where an individualistic society is pushed upon us. Life for some of us is not about being the standout star; I for one love a sense of community.

I always remember my first ever stand-up gig in London. My best mate Rolls and I worked damned hard on our set for weeks and yet we bombed. Zero laughs. It was awful. The taxi back to the hotel was horrendous. The silence was painful, neither of us spoke a word until Rolls piped up and said, 'Imagine if you were doing this on your own.' We had each other and in that moment it fucking mattered.

Time and again we hear about the fact that we all have the potential to be a superhero. Well, maybe it's just as acceptable to be part of the super-team, the supergroup, or the sidekick even. I enjoy my own company but I can get incredibly lonely. In fact, I don't think I'm particularly good for me. I have friends who have gone out on their own, as it's what is expected. Look at every girl/boy band or rock band there's ever been. It's often led by someone 'outwith' the band, whispering in their superstar's ear about how they need to think about themselves for a change. It just so happens the ones doing the whispering will benefit financially though, right? I know for a fact that friends of mine are lonely, at times utterly miserable. But hey, they're 'making it', so who gives a fuck, right? Any other way just wouldn't be 'special' enough. It's just simply too ordinary for some to remain an equal part of something. But this presents us with a problem: if we don't stand out these days, if we're not held up on a pedestal, considered special, then we're simply too ordinary. FFS.

Secularism

Secular societies cease to believe in anything that is bigger than or beyond themselves. I'm not religious but I do believe there is/are things bigger than or beyond me. The planet, the universe, nature. We've all met people who believe they are the most important thing in the world. We all have friends who have made the shift from a loving, caring, friendly human being to a massive world class knobber who is the epitome of the word narcissist. Quite literally in love with him/herself. Social media has created a generation of narcissists. Gerald Sinclair writes, 'People are not concerned with world issues anymore. The majority of us are content spending our free time taking deceptive selfies and editing them in order to make ourselves more attractive so we can post them all over our social media accounts.'

On a lesser level, we can all have moments where our triumphs and failures feel like the be all and end all.

'People tend to think that happiness is a stroke of luck, something that will descend like fine weather if you're fortunate. But happiness is the result of personal effort. You fight for it, strive for it, insist upon it, and sometimes even travel around the world looking for it. You have to participate relentlessly.'

—Elizabeth Gilbert

I'm a huge rugby fan and the New Zealand All Blacks have a wonderful phrase that when translated from Maori means 'Plant Trees You'll Never See'. In other words, it's not about you. It's about what you're creating for the next generation, it's about how you are making things better for them. I love this. It's about your legacy. Too many people are desperate to be the best *in* the world; what if more of us flipped our thinking and strived to be the best *for* the world?

Perhaps just a subtle change of words but this is a game changer.

Romanticism

As soon as we pin our ambitious hopes on finding the perfect partner, 'the one' very quickly can become a lifelong search similar to that of happiness. If we're constantly chasing what the media have portrayed and taught us to strive for then we're going to be left very disappointed with a series of relationships that are 'fine' at best. We get our hopes up even when we know that love tends to creep up when we least expect it. When we expect it, it tends to creep us out. There are very few people out there living a life of regular hot steamy sex and adventure with him/her off the TV. But there are many, *many* happy people living with their best friend in the whole world.

The Media

Imagine the media *not* playing a part in our lives. How would we feel? No news, no newspapers, no social media. I know a guy who hasn't watched or read the news for two years. Not a single TV show or newspaper. He's removed things such as Facebook from his life. He reckons he is significantly happier as a result. I think I might be a little jealous. For those not brave enough to 'switch off', the challenge we face is that the media plays such a massive role in the world and in our lives with a huge focus on things that scare, worry, panic and enrage us. What if we reported on the good stuff? The solutions? Would anyone actually buy a 'Good News' newspaper or watch a show that only reports on how we can help each other and save the planet? As lovely as it sounds, I'm not sure many would pay attention. At the very least though it would regularly remind us that the news we most need to focus on comes from our own lives and direct experiences.

Perfectibility

With our filter-rich modern society we are taught that we can all live a perfect life of success, contentment and, while we're at it, here's how your body and face must look. Even in the non-celebrity side of things, think about the images and news your friends share on their social media. Painting a picture of perfection is 99% of it. Most of it of course will be thought-out, filtered nonsense, much of which leaves us comparing our own lives to that of others and feeling like we're not living our best life. We all have shit going on in our lives, we all have worries, stresses and anxieties. Perfection is not within our reach. Anyone's reach. We need to feel comfortable sharing our real fears, imperfections and vulnerabilities. Finding the people that allow us to do this is more important than claiming your life is as perfect as you pretend it is on Facebook.

There's a huge amount in this modern world causing psychological distress for so many. The cure doesn't lie with spending more time on reading beauty magazines that are proposing 99 ways you can look prettier because obviously you're not pretty enough. Or scrolling miles and miles of Facebook reading the conversations of our Facebook friends who we haven't seen for 20 years and actually aren't really our friends, but we have them on our Facebook anyway. Or trying to replicate the life of a billionaire who in real life isn't happy and looks just like me and you.

Imagine we could remove all the aspects of modern life that makes us feel stressed, anxious, worried, depressed, unhappy, pressured…

What's Up Doc?

'If the world is cold, make it your business to build fires.'

—*Horace Traubel*

Most of you won't know this, but I have a mate called Andy and he's a doctor. Dr Andy Cope. An actual doctor. Well, not a regular doctor. But he is a doctor. He's a doctor of happiness. Yes, really. In fact, he's the UK's first ever doctor of happiness. Dr Happy. Dr Feelgood. Dr Lovejoy. I'll stop now.

So basically he's not the kind of doctor that tells you that you have the common cold. He's way more exciting than that. He's more the kind of doctor who tells you that you have the less common 'Warm'.

Now, I'm not sure if you've heard of the 'Warm' before – it's this thing we all have inbuilt from birth but unfortunately many of us forget how to use it. It's our ability to see good. I don't mean 20/20 vision; to be more specific I mean *the* good, in all we experience. Examples include the Warm in all people, Mondays, work, failure, getting older, all situations. Especially the situation you're in right now. Like, right now.

The 'Warm' gives you the ability to turn things around. A day, a relationship, a career, a life. Aye, you heard…a fucking life. Other people's lives. Anyone's life.

Even yours.

The best bit about the 'Warm' is that's it's hugely infectious. Catching. It spreads with great ease.

The 'Warm' is incredibly easy to diagnose and sufferers tend to spot signs of infection early on. Those closest to you are likely to spot it every bit as quick. In fact, if you've been struck by the Warm it's highly likely that they, too, are experiencing the symptoms.

Among other things these symptoms include smiling, energy, laughter, positivity, the desire to do stuff, fire in your belly, friendliness and the dreaded alternative dance outburst.

So, my mate Andy may not be a real doctor in the medical sense, but in some ways we can *all* be a doctor of happiness.

If we want to.

It's essentially a mindset, a choice. You can, alternatively, wake up every day and choose to see the Cold in everything. Or not.

'I began to realize how important it was to be an enthusiast in life. He taught me that if you are interested in something, no matter what it is, go at it at full speed ahead. Embrace it with both arms, hug it, love it and above all become passionate about it. Lukewarm is no good. Hot is no good either. White hot and passionate is the only thing to be.'

—Roald Dahl

As doctors of happiness we don't need to diagnose anyone with the flu, that's for medical doctors. We could however diagnose the 'Full'. There are no flu jabs here but we could all do with a few more shots of the Full.

Not sure if you're heard of the Full? It's how you feel when life is good. Full heart, full energy, full relationships, a full cup. But not a cup just half full, full to the fucking top. The brim. The white hot and passionate brim.

I'm definitely not suggesting physical check-ups either. Keep your hands to yourself and no sneaky fingers up the bum. Remember, you're not an actual doctor. But definitely massive rockets up the ass.

Not sure if you've ever had a rocket up the ass. Not literally. Not a real one, you'd break. Actually, you'd definitely, 100%, die. A metaphorical rocket of course. Life-changing at worst. As a doctor of happiness you can dish them out. How do we do this? With love, kindness, positivity, energy, respect, enthusiasm and cuddles. Yeah, you heard, cuddles. Cuddles make the world go round. Don't even try and deny it.

Dish out rockets. Rocket cuddles on prescription. Fire them up and point them in all directions.

Rocket cuddles might sound silly but if you Google 'How to be Happy' or 'What Makes People Happy?' then you're going to find millions of pages rammed full of all sorts of weird and wonderful ideas. Some will be perfect for you; some will perhaps be of less help or not particularly up your street and some will be pure happy-clappy tripe.

You're definitely not going to find anything about rocket cuddles but what you will find though across the internet is definite cross-over. There will be some similarities in many of the writings available. Themes will begin to emerge.

Among them themes of simplicity, living in the present, gratitude, kindness, healthy food, sleep and exercise.

Happiness will likely always be treated by most as the pot of gold at the end of the rainbow, the light at the end of the tunnel, as an everlasting chase, a Gumball Rally of sorts, a crazy competition among us all, a race.

There's no chase and there's certainly no race. And the sooner everyone realizes this the better. It's not about how busy we can be or how much money we can make. It's not about the size of your house or the type of car you drive. No one gives a fuck and when you die none of this will be discussed at your funeral. People will be too busy discussing what kind of human you were. You'll either be remembered as one of the good guys, or an asshole.

What I've learned and, in fact, what I'm still learning is that happiness is about doing less and being more. It's about right here, right now.

And we've always known it.

When Two Tribes Go To ~~War~~ Peace

Who's the happiest person you know? Like, properly happy. The one person who just seems to have it all sussed. Once you have someone in mind, think about what makes them so happy…

Let me guess: Stuff just doesn't bother them, they don't worry, they're comfortable with their lot etc. etc. etc. Sounds magic, eh? But hang on a minute, a life of no worry? A life of acceptance? Zero overthinking? Nah, surely not? Seems practically impossible.

Maybe it's not all that difficult.

'Wakan Tanka, Great Mystery, teach me how to trust my heart, my mind, my intuition, my inner knowing, the senses of my body, the blessings of my spirit. Teach me to trust these things so that I may enter my Sacred Space and love beyond my fear, and thus Walk in Balance with the passing of each glorious Sun.'

—Lakota Prayer

The first time I ever saw my dad cry it definitely freaked me out a little. I reckon I was about 10 years old and I can remember thinking something must be very wrong. It turns out quite a lot was wrong.

Historically.

My dad had been reading a book called *Bury My Heart at Wounded Knee.* 'The saddest true story I've ever read,' he told me.

Like, surely it can't be that bad, I thought? I had this strange compulsion to know more. Like many 10-year-olds I had some questions.

My dad told me that the book was told from the Native Americans' perspective. He spoke of a truly saddening story of 'man's inhumanity to man', how they were systematically slaughtered, starved and displaced.

I couldn't believe what my dad was telling me. I had learned a little in school about things such as World War 2 and that was difficult enough to comprehend, but this, this fucked with my 10-year-old mind. It still fucks with my nearly 40-year-old mind. My dad didn't want me to read it so I did what all respectable young kids do when their parents don't want them doing something, I read it anyway.

I didn't read it all. There were bits I found difficult to follow and bits I simply couldn't read because it scared me so much. I literally had to stop reading it at times. Eventually the book disappeared, and it would be many years until I picked up another copy and read it fully.

But when I was 10, I needed to know more about these people. So many different tribes with so many awesome names! There was no Google, so it was off to the library to learn more.

I arrived home with about six books all about the Native Americans, none of which told the true story in the way *Bury My Heart* had done. But there was still much to take in.

I lapped it up, all of it. I became obsessed with all things Native American. The artwork, the writings, the philosophies and the music. To this day I'm not aware of many other 10-year-old boys from Scotland who, instead of posters of footballers on their bedroom walls, had images of Chief Sitting Bull, Black Elk or Luther Standing Bear.

'So tractable, so peaceable are these people that I swear to your Majesties there is not in the world a better nation. They love their neighbours as themselves, and their discourse is ever sweet and gentle, and accompanied with a smile; and though it is true that they are naked, yet their manners are decorous and praiseworthy.'

—Christopher Columbus

These guys spoke so much sense, so why did the cowboys always win and why did everyone want to be the cowboy? Not me, give me my bow and arrow any day and let me be. I couldn't get enough of what I was reading and if it hadn't been for the fact my local library had only six books on the subject then maybe I would have learned so much more.

I think this perhaps odd obsession has helped shape my thinking to this day.

'You have to look deeper, way below the anger, the hurt, the hate, the jealousy, the self-pity, way down deeper where the dreams lie, son. Find your dream. It's the pursuit of the dream that heals you.'

—Billy Mills

I learned all about realizing 'oneness'. I was young, not very good at it, definitely didn't fully understand it, but it got me thinking big time about the world. In fact, scrap that, it got me thinking mahoosively about the whole damn universe. This huge big thing we and everything else is part of. It's all just one thing. That's why it's called uni-verse. One. Including you and me. You are part of the thing. Remember, secularism…Plant Trees You'll Never See. It's not about you.

'The overall commentary on what I'm doing is saying, Hey look! I get to create whatever persona I want to, and it's all up to me. And the truth is, we are all basically the universe—pretending to be humans for a brief moment of time.'

—RuPaul

I learned that the sense of our 'oneness' is something spoken about across all tribes. This sense is very much intuitive and can be developed with practice. Like mindfulness.

It quickly became clear that Native American wisdom was a bit too deep and really rather profound, a little too much so for me at a young age. I have revisited it many times since. I love it.

Experts tell us that in our everyday lives and routines, we encounter this same intuitive feeling of 'oneness', albeit most of the time it's far more subtle. During these moments, 'it's important to not identify this feeling as nonsense and realize that it's our ability to connect with the greater truth of existence on a deeper level'. See what I mean? Deep!

Let's go even deeper still.

Matt Valentine says, 'We are one, like a large organism. And in the same way that organs, tissue, veins, nerves, and the other parts that make up our body can sometimes seem separate, but are always very much an inseparable part of the same one greater system, we, too, are intrinsically connected and should live in a way that we become more and more aware of this interconnected nature and seek to express it in our daily lives. Humans, nature, animals, oceans and so on.'

And, like the Pirahã tribe, this always results in more love, compassion and kindness, resulting in greater peace.

> So, live your life that the fear of death can never enter your heart. Trouble no one about their religion; Respect others in their view, and demand that they respect yours. Love your life, perfect your life, beautify all things in your life.
>
> Seek to make your life long and its purpose in the service of your people. Prepare a noble death song for the day when you go over the great divide. Always give a word or a sign of salute when meeting

or passing a friend, Even a stranger, when in a lonely place. Show respect to all people and grovel to none.

When you arise in the morning give thanks for the food and for the joy of living. If you see no reason for giving thanks, the fault lies only in yourself.

Abuse no one and no thing, for abuse turns the wise ones to fools and robs the spirit of its vision.

When it comes your time to die, be not like those whose hearts are filled with the fear of death, so that when their time comes they weep and pray for a little more time to live their lives over again in a different way. Sing your death song and die like a hero going home.

—Chief Tecumseh (Crouching Tiger) Shawnee Nation 1768–1813

I'm not even going to try and add to this perfect message. I will remind you of this bit though:

'Love your life, perfect your life, beautify all things in your life.'

Perfect *your* life, not someone else's. Not perfect yours in line with what the world tells you. Perfect the life that feels right for you. This is not about achieving perfection.

'I do not think the measure of a civilization is how tall its buildings of concrete are. But rather how well its people have learned to relate to their environment and fellow man.'

—Sun Bear of the Chippewa Tribe

Scotland the Brave

Sun Bear's ancient words are echoed by Scotland's first minister, Nicola Sturgeon. She believes Scotland can play its part in helping to create a 'fairer, happier world' by changing the focus of governments from wealth to well-being. It's fair to say that the economic measure of GDP is often seen as the most important measurement of a country's overall success.

I am incredibly proud that Scotland is leading the way with this currently. Along with New Zealand and Iceland we have established the network of Wellbeing Economy Governments to challenge the acceptance of GDP as the ultimate measure of a country's success.

Sturgeon said:

> GDP measures the output of all of our work but it says nothing about the nature of that work, about whether that work is worthwhile or fulfilling. It puts a value, for example, on illegal drug consumption but not on unpaid care. It values activity in the short term that boosts the economy even if that activity is hugely damaging to the sustainability of our planet in the longer term.
>
> The argument of that group is that the goal, the objective, of economic policy should be collective wellbeing — how happy and healthy a population is, not just how wealthy a population is.

Essentially, we're saying, 'Hey, we want to value the well-being and happiness of our people instead of material "stuff".'

Awesome, right? It's like Sun Bear is backing up this very same ideal, except perhaps in a slightly different sense. In this way, he's describing more our ability to live in harmony with the world around us – both nature and humanity specifically.

So just as we add Scotland, New Zealand and Iceland to the party, let's get this right. For years and years, those that were here way before us – way before we introduced them to religion, greed, advanced weapons, illness and such – lived their lives centred around living in harmony with the world, kindness, happiness, love, respect, simplicity and living in the present.

Well-being, not wealth.

We need to ask ourselves again…are we trying to be the best *in* the world or the best *for* the world?

Imagine…

In Buddhism, it's understood that the best way you can help others is by working on yourself.

This is what's sometimes called 'lighting up your corner of the world' or in other words 'lighting that fucker up for yourself' and it refers to the way you can inspire those you meet by the example you set and how this is more powerful than anything else you can do to help others. It's about how you choose to have impact or not. It's about the you that gets out of bed every single day. Even Mondays. It's how you choose to think. It's your energy, your passion, it's the you that turns up, the you that walks into the room. Every room, full fucking beam.

Remember, your energy introduces you before you do.

To positively inspire and empower others doesn't mean 'make millions, forget your friends, grow your ego and act like a massive dick', this refers to something far more important, bigger, more meaningful. This is about the real you, your true self. But being happy with you. An inner peace if you will. A contentment.

Native American wisdom is both vast and immensely beautiful.

At the start of this section, I quoted a Lakota prayer. It speaks of a Sacred Space. Now you may have your own sacred space. Your home, your bed, your car in the morning, the woods, the beach on holiday but according to Native American wisdom, the Sacred Space is the space between the in-breath and out-breath.

How many times have you heard someone speaking about mindfulness over the last few years? If you're even slightly familiar with it then you'll immediately recognize this as significant.

I was fascinated by this as a kid but of course I didn't really get it. It was many years later when I read *Mindfulness* by Mark Williams that I had a kind of 'this seems familiar' moment and then I remembered, this is a Native American thing too! In fact, it's an *everyone* thing. It doesn't matter what you believe but pretty much every religion, every superhero, every sidekick, yoga, mindfulness, you name it, they all believe that love, peace, being present, showing gratitude, nature, kindness – you get the point – is what makes you, me and the world so fucking special.

Oh, and meditation. Something I'm working hard to get better at. Paying attention to the space between the in-breath and the out-breath, or inhalation and exhalation, is a meditation technique that's been practised for thousands of years.

'The space between breaths is said to be where we enter back into our natural state, where "I" falls away and we exist as "one" with the world around us. It's in releasing the ego, the sense of a separate self, which thinks it's independent when it's really interdependent, that we transcend fear and realize true love.'

I fucking love this. It's not about me. Or you. Or them.

It's about *us*. And *there* is everything wrong with the world today. We're all out to be the best *in* the world.

So once again, here's my challenge to you. What if we were to stop trying to be the best *in* the world and we focused on being the best *for* the world?

Think about it; this changes things. It's a subtle change in the wording but when we really think about it, it's a great big fucking shift and it could change the world. For you. For each other. For everyone and for everything.

It would, according to all the history books, science and psychology cause a great big happiness ripple in the world.

Bill and Ted had it right years ago. 'Be excellent to each other!'

One minor issue is the number of assholes we have in the world and to make matters worse many of them are in charge. Just look at British and American politics right now. Looks who's running the show. It's a shit show.

Are *they* doing all they can to be the best *for* the world? Are they being truly excellent to each other?

I think we know the answer.

But we can be.

You and me.

Remember, it starts with you.

Plant trees you'll never see.

CHAPTER 6

Confidently Lost

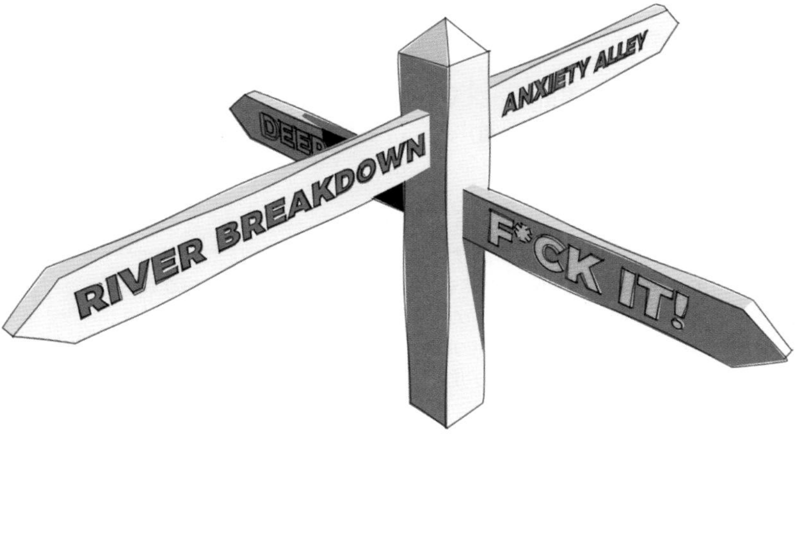

Sometimes things go wrong. Even humans.

They say everyone has a chapter they don't read out loud.

Here's mine, written out loud.

Think of it as the hidden track on your favourite album from back in the day when albums were so awesome they had a 7–10 minute period of silence after the last track. And then just after you'd finally fallen asleep…you were rudely awoken by a mysterious noise that would lead you into a weird and wonderful world that left you feeling uneasy, yet strangely at peace.

But with questions…

So many questions.

I'm looking at you Billy Joe Armstrong from Green Day. You and that drummer of yours with your 80-second acoustic ditty that you appear to have written just for me.

'Everyone doesn't need access to you. Some people are draining and they don't even know it. You're allowed to say no, you're allowed to not answer calls, you're allowed to break plans, and if you need to save yourself do it.'

—Sylvester McNutt III

I wrote the following in April, 2018.

I'm in Aviemore on holiday with my family and some dear friends.

For those who have never heard of Aviemore, it's in the highlands of Scotland and it's incredibly beautiful.

It's April and I am looking at the most stunning scenery Scotland has to offer. Snow-topped mountains, heather-clad fields, deer, sheep and to top it all off the snow is falling heavily.

There's not a breath of wind and not a sound to be heard. I can see for miles and through the snow-filled valleys the stars are littered across the sky, shining as bright as I've ever seen.

It's like a postcard. Perfect.

The thing is…

It's 4 a.m.

I'm in a hot tub.

Alone.

I haven't slept for over a month.

And I can't stop crying.

The only thing that I know for sure right now is the hot tub is helping. I feel safer in here. Safer physically, safer mentally and safer emotionally. I feel lighter. Floaty. It seems to bring a temporary reprieve of sorts.

A temporary reprieve from what, I'm not actually really sure.

I've no idea what this is, I don't really understand what's happening. All I know is that I'm in my late 30s and never before have I felt so scared, so lonely, so vulnerable, so tired, so fearful, so short of breath, so overwhelmed, so isolated and so sore.

Everything aches.

Fuck, it sounds dramatic.

All hope seems to have gone, like my world is ending. I want to scream, cry, hide and never go anywhere again.

I feel like I have lost control, like I am going to explode. Not explode in anger, I mean literally, like I am actually going to explode.

I feel like I have lost me.

I *am* lost.

Lost with a hysterical feeling of urgency.

I can't switch it off.

Waiting for it to pass. Always waiting.

Why am I feeling like this?

What the fuck is happening?

I'm going to have to ask for help.

But no one will understand.

'And something inside me just...broke. That's the only way I could describe it.'

—*Ranata Suzuki*

And there we have it, friends. Something inside me just...broke.

I mentioned in Chapter 2 that occasionally we might have a nightmare in attempting to achieve our dreams. In 2018, this was to be my year. I had worked hard for this moment; dreams were coming true.

Just one minor issue, behind closed doors, I was having one almighty nightmare and I've never spoken about it publicly.

Until now.

Looking back now I can see where it began, I can track it back. I was probably 9–12 months leading into it and 9–12 months coming out of it. If I'm being completely honest, I've still got a way to go.

It started out as butterflies and then it began to hurt.

As I sat there in the hot tub writing stuff down, I was trying to work out how I could explain to my wife what exactly it was that I was feeling. It had got to such a stage that I was going to have to say something. I needed to sit her down and somehow put it into words, lay it all out and just hope that she understood. She knew I hadn't been myself for a while, but things had taken a turn. My bright happy world had quickly gotten a lot darker.

I had managed to keep it all in and share it with no one. I was beginning to feel it seeping out of me. People had begun to notice that I wasn't quite 'on it'. During the particularly bad spells I would take some time off work here and there, putting it down to a bad cold but it's very hard when you've been booked to speak at someone's annual conference, and you need to be razor sharp, the 'star turn'.

I tried to work out how to put it across to people so I wouldn't sound silly. '*I keep on feeling like I'm going to explode*' wasn't going to cut it for me, I needed to do better, so I kept writing stuff down. My thinking was that if I kept putting down on paper how I was feeling along with all the things that were troubling me then maybe I could think of a way to communicate to my loved ones that I wasn't feeling too great.

I wrote down the following...

> It doesn't seem to matter what I say or do, I can't shift this feeling. I'm on holiday and I feel like I'm trapped in my own body and can't get out.
>
> I think I've just got to go through it. There's no way to switch it off. I've got to go through it, there's no other way around it. I've got to go through it.

I read it back and all I could think of in this moment was the 1989 children's picture book *We're Going on a Bear Hunt* written by Michael Rosen. It momentarily brought a smile to my face, a giggle almost.

Even though I was quite familiar with the book, I felt the urge to Google it. I read it from start to finish. It doesn't last long.

In the hot tub, over and over in my mind I just kept reading the book's most famous lines 'I can't go over it, I can't go under it. Oh no! I've got to get through it!' Again, I was smiling. And crying, still fucking crying.

This was actually a minor breakthrough moment for me. I *had* to go through it. Everything I've ever read says the same. Accept it, acknowledge it, welcome it, doff one's cap to it. You can't just tell your mental health to fuck off and all is back to normal.

We're going on a bear hunt.
We're going to catch a big one.
What a beautiful day!
We're not scared.
Uh-uh! Grass!
Long wavy grass.
We can't go over it.
We can't go under it.
Oh no!
We've got to go through it!

Reproduced by permission of Walker Books Ltd

That first page makes me think about the effort that goes into getting out of bed. Doing everything I can to be as positive as possible about the day ahead. Trying to see the beauty in things and trying my utmost to be brave.

But when my anxiety is firing on all cylinders there's always something that gets in the way, tripping me up. Something miniscule, something silly. In the book it's grass but in my head it might be a meeting, but then it builds and builds inside my head, snowballing. In the book the grass turns into a river, then mud, then a forest and before you know it, a full-on snowstorm.

In my head, a shit storm. A shit storm of worry, fear, panic and pain.

In the book they keep on going. Trudging through each obstacle, every hurdle, getting dirtier, wetter, colder, more lost.

As I read *Going on a Bear Hunt* I couldn't help but connect the young family's adventures with my own. I keep going too, taking on each and every hurdle, feeling colder and more lost along the way.

The further away from home they get, the more lost they feel. The closer to the bear they get, the scarier it becomes. Like going to work. Or a party.

I can recall sitting in the hot tub reading this book and wondering if anyone else has ever interpreted it in this way before?

Eventually the kids meet the bear. Naturally they shit themselves and run.

The family run home, back across all the obstacles they've already faced, followed by the bear.

Quick! Back through the cave! Tiptoe! Tiptoe! Tiptoe!

Back through the snowstorm! Hoooo wooooo! Hoooo wooooo!

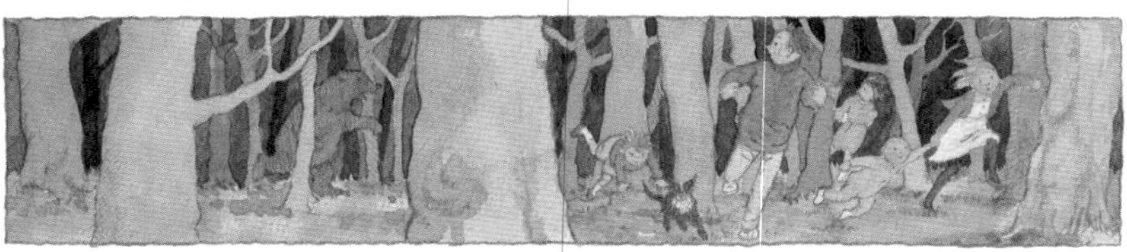

Back through the forest! Stumble trip! Stumble trip! Stumble trip!

Back through the mud! Squelch squerch! Squelch squerch!

Back through the river! Splash splosh! Splash splosh! Splash splosh!

Back through the grass! Swishy swashy! Swishy swashy!

This for me pretty much sums up a day in the life of anxiety. Even once I've fought my way through my day, each and every part of it ruminates around my head as I relive each detail, going back through it again and again, questioning all of it, wondering and worrying if I could have done it better, hoping it doesn't get me again.

Finally, the children arrive home, shut the bear out of the house, lock the front door, run up the stairs and all hide under the duvet saying, 'We're not going on a bear hunt again.'

Get to our front door.
Open the door.
Up the stairs.

Oh no!
We forgot to shut the door.
Back downstairs.

Shut the door.
Back upstairs.
Into the bedroom.

Into bed.
Under the covers.

When I was at my lowest point I just wanted to hide in my bed. But I couldn't settle, as soon as I climbed into bed I'd be up again, pacing, always pacing, in bed, out of bed, struggling to calm my mind down.

At the end of the book, the bear is pictured traipsing dejectedly on a beach at night, suggesting to the reader that he's still out there, and not gone forever, as one might hope…

For many months after my hot tub experience, and even occasionally now, I can feel it. Just like the bear at the end of the story, it's gone but it's not really gone, it's out there. It's in me.

It's not my favourite book of all time, it's no *Hungry Caterpillar* and it's definitely not *Where the Wild Things Are*. But I've always liked it, my kids loved it and in this moment, I couldn't stop reading it.

It was helping.

The Scottish Highlands – as beautiful as they are – couldn't fix me. The starry, snow-filled skies couldn't cut it.

But, weirdly, 4 a.m. hot tubs and *We're Going on a Bear Hunt* appeared to be aiding my perspective.

Is this kid's book just another story of adventure and mischief or is it – in a weird and mysterious way – actually a metaphor for dealing with anxiety? My eyes kept running down over the same four lines, over and over again.

> We can't go over it.
>
> We can't go under it.
>
> Oh no!
>
> We've got to go through it!

The lovely folks over at Walker Books very kindly granted me permission to share with you some of their now legendary and classic book. We're told that even though there are literally thousands of licensed 'Bear Hunt' products around the world, this is most definitely the first time it's been used to highlight the struggles of living with anxiety.

For the purpose of clarity, I don't know if I was having a nervous breakdown. I think I was and if I wasn't then I was 100% dipping more than just a toe in the water. My foot was well and truly submerged. Scrap that, I'm pretty sure I had a full leg in the waters of River Breakdown. I never actually received professional help. Maybe I should have. I sure felt like I was having a nervous breakdown. And if I wasn't then OMFG, I don't ever want to because this, this was fucking shit.

Who am I kidding? Even now I'm struggling to just write it. I'm trying to dress it up and play it down.

I've just realized this is the first time I've actually properly acknowledged publicly I was having some kind of breakdown. I've never said this out loud to anyone. Writing this down actually feels OK.

Fuck, here goes….

In 2018, I had a nervous breakdown.

Wish List

- Peace of mind

To Anxiety and Beyond

Now, I'm not a doctor, I'm not an expert on mental health and I certainly don't claim to be, but I can tell you these four things for certain:

1. Anxiety fucking sucks. Like, so much.
2. *We're Going on a Bear Hunt* almost perfectly depicts a day in the life of a nervous breakdown. Oh my fucking fuck is it accurate!
3. Anxiety is not a mental illness. Fact.
4. If you struggle with anxiety, you're going to be alright.

Now, point number 4 is definitely going to be the hardest one to accept if you're not doing too great just now. But it's true, you're going to be alright.

No one will get it. Unless they've been there, no one will know how you're feeling. Some of them will try and help you. Some of them will even be successful at it. But what I have learned is this…

It's down to you. People are great but this, this is on you.

Bear in mind, anxiety disorder is *not* a mental illness, it is a behavioural condition, there is a very big difference.

Mental illnesses are clinical conditions which have a 'biological' basis, anxiety disorders are caused by a 'resetting' of the 'baseline' anxiety level; this happens through reinforcing the anxiety disorder by repetitive anxious behaviour.

Darlene Lancer says 'anxiety is the apprehension of experiencing fear in the future.'

So, to paint a bigger picture for you here. I had recently announced to the world that I was putting on 'The biggest event of inspiration for young people ever to be held in Scotland'. I called it 'Fire Up Scotland' and it was billed as 'The rock show of inspirational events'. We would have 12,000 tickets on offer, for free. The best line-up of speakers and performers, like no other careers event ever before. This event would change lives.

Whilst I had surrounded myself with some of the most lovely, skilled and supportive people in the business, in my mind at this time, it was just me, on my own. The event was still six months away, the line-up was looking great and with the help of a few very generous people I had raised almost enough money. I had worked on this for 18 months.

It was nothing but excitement all the way.

Then suddenly, all I could think was…

> What if no one signs up?
>
> What if only 100 people sign up?
>
> What if I can't raise the money?
>
> What if?
>
> What if?
>
> What if?

Almost the same questions as in Chapter 1.

Then within 24 hours of going public every single one of the 12,000 tickets was snapped up. We had to close the website down.

Normally I'd be celebrating but when the call came in all I could think was…

> What if it's shit?
>
> What if no one turns up?
>
> What will it do to my career?
>
> What if it fails?
>
> What if?
>
> What if?
>
> What if?

With anxiety, the danger that is feared isn't normally imminent – it may not even be known or realistic. Look at my questions above. Most of these are based on the unknown. I was freaking out even before we even announced the event to the public. I had all the right people around me and almost the right amount of money. And when those questions were answered and the worries alleviated, I created more.

But my brain was bursting. This wonderfully positive thing I was trying to do with other likeminded people proved to be the trigger. Even typing this right now I can feel it in my chest; this is how I know it was the trigger of all of this. Any mention of it, any reference to it and I can feel it. It's actually nothing to do with the event itself but in my mind it became *all* about the actual event itself.

'Stop thinking about everything so much. You are breaking your own heart.'

—Anon

I always try to remember that we need anxiety. It's part of what makes us human, it's there for a reason, it keeps us alive. The reality is some have it at a low level and some have it real bad. Most of the time I have low level but there are moments when it fucking explodes. And in 2018, it well and truly exploded.

In contrast, typically, fear is an emotional and physical reaction to a present, known threat. I had recently been told by an industry 'expert' that I couldn't pull off such an event and that others had failed before me. I received a call from a friend telling me that there had been a few malicious remarks made about me and my event by some people I respected and looked up to in the industry.

Until this moment it was nothing but positives, of course it would work, nothing but possibilities. But as I approached my deadline for going public, I realized that not everyone was going to have my back. I was privy to a few more comments that had been made about me and what I was attempting to do. A little seed of doubt had been well and truly planted.

This kind of thing has never really bothered me but this time the seed of doubt just grew and grew and grew.

In this moment I learned a very valuable lesson about people. And it's this…

No matter how hard you work, no matter how kind you are, no matter how good your intentions are, no matter how good you actually are at what you do and no matter how hard you try, sometimes, sometimes your face simply doesn't fit.

So, I learned to just crack on and make it work with my own fucking face.

Lancer teaches us that 'Anxiety is often accompanied by obsessive worry and an inability to concentrate that may affect our sleep. It can trigger a full-blown fight-flight-or-freeze response of our sympathetic nervous system that prepares us to meet real danger. However, a big difference between fear and anxiety is that because anxiety is an emotional response to something that hasn't occurred, there is nothing to fight or flee.'

I kept trying to tell myself this, that everything was OK, but the tension just kept on building up inside my body. There appeared to be absolutely no action I could take to release it. Instead, my mind went round and round, replaying possibilities and scenarios. Snowballing again.

This is why I was sore and felt like I was going to explode. And exactly the reason I couldn't sleep. Until this point I had never before experienced difficulty with sleep. Wow, is it hard-going.

There is literally no other cause for anxiety disorders. All of the symptoms I was experiencing were caused by maladjusted reactions in my brain causing my mind and body to react with a horrendous level of anxiety.

What makes it harder is that society pigeon-holes conditions and, because there is no pigeon-hole for anxiety as such, it gets labelled as 'mental illness', or the anxious among us are dismissed as 'neurotic' or 'hypochondriacs'. We are at times encouraged to toughen up, get over it or man up. I began to freak out that I was losing my mind. I began to believe I was seriously ill and there was no way back.

But still I kept it to myself.

It started to impact upon my job and my family, it was becoming more apparent to the people closest to me that I wasn't doing so great. I did a pretty good job at covering it up – all those years performing were now paying off. Most spotted nothing!

Mental illness is very specific and research tells us it can't be treated through behavioural treatments alone – they require medicinal treatments also. Anxiety disorder does not require any medicinal intervention, which is why psychologists have been treating anxiety disorders with psychotherapy for decades; it just falls short of providing a complete solution.

You see, anxiety disorders are not at all related to mental illness, they are caused by a misfiring of the emotion of fear – by preventing that 'misfire' you can completely erase anxiety disorders, their symptoms and every thought, obsession, phobia, compulsion or anxious focus they cause.

Fear, what an absolute asshole you can be.

As I wrote in an earlier chapter, my adventures with fear began when I was five but they truly kicked in when I was 10.

And I know why. Because of a plane crash.

You might remember the Lockerbie air disaster. Never before had I seen images on the television of an exploded plane lying on top of a small Scottish village, a matter of miles from my house.

Man, those images haunted me as a kid. It freaked me right out. Scottish accents like mine on the news. How could this happen? Why would someone plant a bomb on a plane? And those people, their photos appearing on the news, more and more of them each day. The families gathering, the crying. It gave me nightmares.

'When I was a boy and I would see scary things in the news my mother would say to me... "Look for the helpers. You will always find people who are helping".'

—Fred Rogers

The media strikes again. This story got me good and proper. It triggered something that I've never really been able to shake off. A constant worry. An underlying fear of what might go wrong. All – I think – from one news story.

The following summer my family and I headed to Florida for the first time. Mum and Dad had saved for years to give us this magical experience. But I would need to get on a plane. I made myself ill. For weeks building up to getting on that plane I had the worst stomach pains and nausea I'd ever had. The entire flight I was back and fore the toilet, pacing up and down the aisle on the plane. My mum and dad were so worried about me.

Then, for three full weeks travelling around the USA, I was often unwell, except when I was in a swimming pool. Strangely, being in water was helping. I felt safer there. I felt lighter. Floaty. There's a theme here!

To this day I have the same constant worry, the same underlying fear of what might go wrong. I can go months and barely notice it and then out of nowhere it's like it's here on its holidays and it plans on seeing all the sights. I can't sleep, I can't eat, I can't settle. I can't breathe.

But I have lots of baths.

My job helps me immensely. I am fortunate that I get to travel the world and speak in front of the most wonderful audiences. The constant sharing of information around positivity, mindset and fun serves as a daily reminder that I have to try hard to ensure I'm giving myself all the right chances to increase my own happiness.

Literally my whole career, whether it be in the classroom, a comedy club or a conference, I can be found pacing around backstage wondering why the fuck I put myself through this. Thoughts such as 'I could have a normal job' pop into my head regularly along with 'What if they hate me?', 'What if it doesn't work?' and 'I wish that I was good enough.'

Then I get on stage and I am instantly reminded that 'this is why I do it!' and I absolutely love being on stage. There is something quite extraordinary about the immediacy of performing. In front of a live audience you have to be present, you have to be in the moment and you have no opportunity to let your mind wander to the million other 'what if's'. Some of my happiest times have been on stage. That's not to say it doesn't sometimes go wrong; it definitely does. And trust me, then my thoughts go into overdrive.

But even when it goes well I still doubt myself. I have very little confidence in myself. I worry so much about letting people down and when I do, I don't sleep for a very long time.

In school, in university, in work, in meetings, conferences, awards do's and every single party I've ever been to, I feel like I don't fit. Ever.

It's fucking horrendous at times.

'What screws us up the most in life is the picture in our head of how it's supposed to be.'

—Anon

Purpose Fuels Passion

Ahh, welcome to my mind, ladies and gentlemen. That's right, me, Gavin Oattes the motivational speaker. The author of self-help books. The over-thinker, the worrier, the entrepreneur who is also well and truly imposter syndromed up to his eyeballs. That's me. The dude that shits himself regularly. Not literally of course.

This chapter is called 'Confidently Lost' for a reason. When I'm in the zone, doing what I do best, on stage, present, in the moment, I am unbelievably confident and it's real.

Off stage, mingling, chatting with audience members, clients and conference-goers, I'm uncomfortable. On edge. Lost. I find networking events excruciating. I speak for a living and yet I don't know what to say.

As a comedian I have done some outrageous things on stage. Confidence pouring out of me, loud, in your face and at times hugely offensive. Nothing bothers me up there. In reality, I'm painfully shy, socially awkward, anxious and would far rather be at home with my family watching movies and cuddling my cat.

And yet....the stage keeps calling me. The lure of a live audience sets my soul on fire. My passion to help people feel inspired, happy, confident, brave, courageous, fun, creative, never wanes.

And here lies the importance of purpose. Now, everyone is talking about purpose these days, especially in business. I think they think it's new – it's not, it's just that it's in right now, it's a buzz word.

But I'm delighted they're discussing it. I work with CEOs and businesses every day to help them find, shape and deliver on their purpose and I see the difference it makes. Purpose works miracles.

For us as individuals I believe it's even more important to find our purpose. My purpose is to make a difference. There's a reason why – aside from my family – my two biggest passions in life are teaching and comedy. They make a difference. A proper fucking difference. Think about the greatest teachers you ever had as a kid. Entertaining, enlightening, educating. What a skill! Is it learned or does it just come naturally to some?

Who cares?! My whole life I've wanted to work out how I can do just those things to help others to help themselves.

Now think about the awful teachers you had. Bored, miserable, unhappy, negative people. Fuck them. How dare they even enter the classroom. Their job is quite literally to inspire and energize a generation. They need to turn up. Like, TURN UP.

Now think about all the employers you've had, team leaders, managers, etc. It's the same. The ones with a real sense of purpose just stand out, head and shoulders above the rest.

They turn up, because they give a fuck.

For the whole of 2018 I still gave a fuck and I still turned up for my clients, my colleagues and, most importantly, my family. My purpose remained intact, but I learned just how easy it is for a human to break.

I learned it can happen to anyone at any time.

I was so unwell my entire body broke out in hives. Just think about that, hives. This had happened once before when I lost my dad but never across my whole body. I was covered but thankfully not on my face, so once again, I could hide it.

I'm not going to lie, I feel a sense of embarrassment, shame, stupidity and I am genuinely worried about including this chapter in the book. But as always, my purpose is to make a difference, to help others help themselves. That's why this chapter is in. If it helps one other human, in any way whatsoever, then I'm all good.

And if anyone out there wants to judge me negatively or view me as weak, then please put the book down now and pass it to someone else.

I finished 2018 feeling so much better. Fire Up Scotland was a huge success and every week since I've been asked by at least one person when the next one will be. Honestly? I'm not sure I can, but maybe one day I'll feel the time is right.

That day was an extraordinary day. In the end we had almost 10,000 young people in a room and the energy was electric. I found the day very difficult to get through personally, but I was on hosting duties so I made sure I turned up.

But it was one particular tweet that put everything into perspective for me. The very next night, I received a message from a parent.

It read as follows...

> My son has gone through years of not believing he was a success at school. Last night, after Fire Up Scotland, he was a different guy. He spoke for hours about "people like him"! Thank you Gavin, a difference was made yesterday, it mattered...

This one tweet makes it all worthwhile.

Purpose wins.

If we can hold on to something that lights us up then we can be magic again, we can be well again. Find your magic and turn it on. Turn it all the way up, all the way on. To eleven.

To the worriers...

The day will come when you can catch your breath again and notice the trees once more. You'll be able to sit still, move comfortably, listen to an entire album without needing a break. You'll feel glad all over and you'll feel the urge to live like you used to.

And if you ever need someone to talk to, please get in touch.

CHAPTER 7

Unfuck Yourself

"It's ok to lose your shit sometimes because if you keep your shit, you'll end up full of shit and you'll explode and there'll be shit everywhere. A shit storm. And nobody wants that."

—Anon

So, the entire last chapter wasn't ever meant to be a thing. It happened by accident. I questioned even putting it in the book! I wrote it down – which felt good – but then began to worry about other people's perceptions. But after speaking to a few people and getting the opinion of those I know care about me the most, I decided to go for it!

But it wouldn't be right for me to just share with you some of the stuff that went wrong in my head. It's only fair that I share with you what I did about it. Everything in this chapter helped me. Much of it still does. It won't necessarily all work for you but if one thing can help you or a loved one through a shit time then I'm doing something right.

We all have shit days, of course we do. But some of us have shit weeks, shit months and even shit years. But I believe we always have a choice in life. I also believe in magic. It's not always easy but the important question here is this…

Same old shit? Or, crazy new shit?

I was tired from feeling the way I did. It's exhausting. The fake smiles, the suppressed appetite, the going about your daily life pretending you're OK. And in my case getting up in front of an audience every single day, digging so fucking deep to deliver the best performance I possibly could. No one could know. It would make me look weak.

But I *was* weak, not *because* I struggle with anxiety but because I *struggle* with anxiety…I hope that makes sense.

I've learned there's no shortcut. It took me months to even begin feeling better and I will become a better person for it.

So here's what I did about it. Here's how I got my wee piece of magic back…

'You know what the issue is with this world? Everyone wants a magical solution to their problem, and everyone refuses to believe in magic.'

—Alice in Wonderland, by Lewis Carroll

Basically, this section should really be called 'Shit to do when you feel like your world is caving in, you can't stop worrying and you feel like you're about to explode.'

Catchy huh?

So, here goes…

Shit to Do When You Feel Like Your World Is Caving In, You Can't Stop Worrying and You Feel Like You're About to Explode

1. Find Your 'Shove' (Less Sympathy, More Symphony)

Everyone says it, few do it. Every mental health charity, every mental health spokesperson and every single mental health campaign tells us the same thing, TALK TO SOMEONE. And yet it's just so fucking hard. It feels so embarrassing. The last thing you want to be is that negative person who no one wants to be around. But this is different, this is your health and well-being. This is your happiness, you're not being negative, you're reaching out for help.

To be clear: This is NOT you becoming a fucking asshole! You will be amazed just how willing others are to help you during tough times.

They tell us it's OK to not be OK. Well, it's also OK to feel shite.

I'm lucky I have my wife Ali. She's amazing. She listens *and* kicks my ass all at the same time. But kicks my ass in the most positive, loving and 'exactly what Gavin needs' kind of way. She picks me up and gives me just the right amount of 'shove' in the right direction.

This is the very woman who, whilst lying on the surgeon's table after 25 hours of labour, took my hand and told me I was going to be OK. She told *me* I was going to be OK!

Strongest person I know.

Ali's a world-class teacher, an outstanding mum and a phenomenally skilled musician. She says all the right things in the right way at the right time. Just as all great mums and teachers do. And just how a natural musician plays, all the right notes in the right order at the right time, with feeling. Occasionally they improvise. And they mean it, always.

Ali's less sympathy, more symphony. And this is where my inspiration for this chapter comes from. It's about building from the ground up. It's about capturing the right energy and directing it for good. Allowing yourself to draw on all the different sources of help and inspiration. I've no idea if this makes sense to you and I'm even guessing that when Ali reads this, she's going to wonder what the fuck I'm on but trust me, this shit works. So, find your 'shove', whoever they might be.

And remember, less sympathy, more symphony.

The definition for 'symphony' is...

> ***symphony***
> *noun*
> An elaborate musical composition for full orchestra, typically in four movements, at least one of which is traditionally in sonata form.

The official definition for sympathy is…

> ***sympathy***
> *noun*
> Feelings of pity and sorrow for someone else's misfortune.

Read them again, which one excites you the most? Which one is going to help you kick the shit out of life and fill you back up with magic? Pity and sorrow, or an elaborate musical composition for a full orchestra?

I'll say it again; less sympathy, more symphony.

Just so you understand, I'm talking about going all-out full orchestra on your ass. Building your team, your gang.

Your clan.

Full. Fucking. Orchestra.

Now don't get me wrong, we all want, need and deserve a little sympathy from time to time. We naturally forgive failings in others out of sympathy – in fact, we'll dish it out in abundance when it's not ourselves. But when it *is* ourselves, it's all about how we channel it. We definitely need to cut ourselves some slack every now and then, but when we're feeling low, we need energy, movement, passion and that wee piece of magic.

During my toughest days I gave myself a hard time. My self-talk was anything but gentle. This was coming from a place of embarrassment and trying my very best to 'man up'. Other times I found myself wallowing and this is not a helpful place to be.

Ali got the balance right with me and this taught me that I needed to get better at doing the same for myself. And for the record, at no point did 'manning up' help. It was more a case of tuning up.

The best symphonies feature lots of instruments with many different energies, It's no different with people. You need to speak to different types of people that each offer something different, but together they combine to create your own masterpiece.

I have spoken to so few people about my struggles with anxiety. Probably because I don't feel there are too many I could speak to. Some will be surprised to read this because for the main part I've been able to hide it so well.

I also have my mum. She's the second part of my symphony. I can speak to her about anything.

Mum is crazy. Completely and unashamedly cuckoo. And I love her for that. She gives exactly zero fucks at all about anything other than the stuff that matters in life. She's an ex PE teacher from Glasgow who smokes cigars and boy does she speak her mind. Always positive, she's pure west coast magic. One part terrifying and two parts gallusness personified.

Lost her dad when she was 13, lost her husband (my dad) to cancer when she was 60, lost her best friend to cancer when she was 61, and kicked her very own cancer's ass at 62. One hundred per cent brave and *all* mum. She listens to me. And I love her for that.

Then there's Dougie. I work with Dougie. We run a business together. We were thrown together by a previous employer and somehow over time became business partners. Like all the best partnerships, on paper it shouldn't work, but it does. We come from very different backgrounds with very different upbringings. We're trouble together but in a good way. He's old school, I'm new school. He's pies, chips and football, I'm charcuterie, olives and running. But I love him. Like, actually love him. It's an odd relationship. We don't hang out, we never socialize but I can tell him anything.

He's the first person I phoned when my dad died because he'd know what to do. He'd make everything OK. And he did just that. During my worst lows with my anxiety I speak to Dougie. He listens, he doesn't judge. He effectively coaches me through it.

Like Ali and my mum, he doesn't give me too much sympathy, but lots of little 'shoves' when needed.

Symphonies are mostly in four parts. My symphony of people is finished off by my dad.

My dad died in 2012. He's gone but I can still tell him anything. I can still ask him for help, for advice. We have some splendid conversations and I can always ask, 'What would Dad do?'

Fuck I miss him.

Talk to someone. Sit with someone. Hug someone. Find those that will listen, pick you up and dust you down. Talk to those that will allow you to express exactly how you are feeling. It's not always the most obvious people, welcome them in.

And if you get it wrong and they dismiss you, hurt you, mock you, then you tell them to fuck right off.

Notice the people who make an effort to stay in your life.

Friends are great, but only a select few are going to be with you when you are up the whole night crying and need help, it is only going to be someone who genuinely loves you.

2. Write Shit Down

Nowadays we live in a digital world of to-do list apps and Google Docs. The 6000-year-old practice of putting pen to paper is sadly losing its appeal.

Writing stuff down just helps. In my teens I filled notebooks with comedy sketches, stories *and* well, my emotions. Just getting it out, getting it down on paper brings a sense of relief. But there's proper science behind this stuff.

If you don't write things down, your mind spends more time 'paper shuffling' and the fucker creates its own anxiety.

Just like having too many internet tabs open on your laptop at once, sometimes it feels like your brain has done the same thing. It's often the result of trying to mentally juggle too many thoughts or tasks at the same time.

Your brain is like a hard drive. A multilayered, super-epic, crazily complex hard drive. And to make matters worse, it lies to us. I'm sure we'd love to know that our brain is our friend, but it's not. It's tricking us all the time. Even in important moments, our brains are not as good at creating accurate memories as we think they are. There will be memories from your childhood that simply aren't true, but you remember them clearly.

Your brain can help you to convince yourself you were awesome at something when in actual fact you were fucking shit. Or quite the opposite, it can make you feel like a fraud when in actual fact you are fully deserving of all the recognition you are receiving.

And of course, it can make you scared of things that will never happen, or at the very least are incredibly unlikely to happen. Remember from earlier my fear of flying? I've never been scared of heart disease and yet I'm from Scotland. My chances of dying from heart disease are far higher than being on a plane blown up in a terrorist attack. But hey, for a time I wasn't concerned about my diet but was entirely convinced I shouldn't be getting on a plane.

The Zeigarnik effect says we tend to hang on to things in our mind if we don't finish what we start. Writing down your ideas, thoughts and emotions gets them out of your head, freeing up your mental space. It allows your brain to unload some baggage, preventing you from crashing your own precious mental browser.

It might even help you to relax.

There are no notifications popping up to distract you. A proper physical notebook or journal means no emails pinging in, no Facebook updates and no phone calls. Your thumbs can have a rest from the endless scrolling.

You'll remember more. In 2014, the Association of Psychological Science reported that students who physically took notes received a memory boost – particularly when compared to those who took notes via a laptop.

You can write anything down. Bright ideas that pop into your head. Goals that you want to achieve today or for the week ahead. One-liner reminders. To-Do list. To-Done list. Your little nuggets of wisdom and 'ah-ha's'. All the things buzzing around in your brain. Anything keeping you up at night. Your hopes, your dreams, your goals, and aspirations. Your fears, anxieties, and concerns. You get the idea.

Writing things down is a powerful and useful habit. Even if you throw it away, you still get the benefits.

Writing Challenge

I dare you to buy yourself a lovely new notepad. A proper one. One that takes your breath away when you see it. (Tweet me a picture please to @gavinoattes)

OK, so here's your challenge to get you started. All I want you to do for one week is write a three-word happy story to describe your day.

That's it, just three words. Just before bed, create quite literally a three-word happy story about your day.

If you feel the need to keep writing then I dare you to keep going.

3. Don't Just Sing Along, Commit

I've always been a huge fan of music. From a young age I have been in awe of anyone who can sing and play a musical instrument. As a child I loved sitting trying to record the charts on my cassette player. For the younger readers, ask your parents!

I was a teenager in the 1990s and as I mentioned in Chapter 2, it was all about the bands. Britpop was in full swing and Grunge had well and truly arrived. I spent many a night with my headphones on being transported to a place in my imagination that made me feel spectacular.

I miss being 16 and buying a physical album, putting it on and reading the lyrics from the little booklet that was inside the box. I miss reading the artists' notes, all the people they had to thank. The messages for those who have shaped the album and the shout-outs to us, the fans.

Listening to music is a universally enjoyable activity for most people. But it's so much more than just a bit of fun. There are many mental health benefits that come from listening to music. Whether you're stressed, depressed, or even unable to sleep well, music can alleviate negative symptoms and improve your mood.

My drive to work in the morning is like my own sell-out stadium show. Volume is up and fuck me am I Freddie Mercury!

I don't just sing along, I commit.

I *am* Freddie Mercury, or David Bowie, or Debbie Harry, or Mick Jagger, or Paul Stanley, or Marie Fredriksson (Yes, I love Roxette) or whoever the fuck I want to be. I'm pretty much my own Live Aid concert but way more selfish in that I'm helping myself. And it feels incredible. It can be the lyrics, the melody, the riffs, the vocals, if it gets you it gets you.

I'm almost certain I don't need to tell you of the healing properties contained in your favourite songs and albums. You'll have a favourite for all occasions. There are songs out there that pick me up almost instantaneously and there are those that I can have a good cry to.

'One good thing about music, when it hits you, you feel no pain.'

—Bob Marley

We all know that research has proved the benefits of listening to music; it improves our mental well-being but it also boosts our physical health.

'If people take anything from my music, it should be motivation to know that anything is possible as long as you keep working at it and don't back down.'

—Eminem

Music makes us happier, fact. It relieves stress and anxiety. Music therapy can alleviate depression with wonderful benefits to our self-esteem and interpersonal skills. Certain types of music can increase our ability to concentrate and listening to music actually helps us to sleep better.

I go to sleep every night with my headphones on; currently it's my Roger Waters live album, *In the Flesh*. Music lifts our mood, reduces pain, pumps us up and motivates us. It keeps our brains healthy and can help Alzheimer's patients to remember things. It even reduces road rage, especially if you're lost in your own sell-out stadium show!

Or if you get the chance to go and see a live concert, take it! Unlike sport where half the crowd leaves disappointed, everyone leaves happy.

Got a night to yourself? Perfect. Headphones on, phone off, volume up, eyes closed, world off and away you go.

Bliss.

4. Channel Your Inner Goose – Create Uplift

We humans can learn loads of incredible stuff from geese. Yes, geese! Take a 'gander' below…(Gander? Anyone? As you were.)

Geese are among the most incredible creatures on earth. A collective group of geese is commonly known as a gaggle BUT only when they are on land. In the air they are known as a skein, team or my particular favourite, a wedge of geese. And in the sky is where they truly come into their own, outperforming other birds. They are the New Zealand All Blacks/Team SKY/Emergency Services/A-Team of birds and there are some pretty incredible reasons why many successful people in the world are citing the simple goose as their inspiration.

Put it this way, if you want to be the best human you can possibly be, then you need to learn to channel your inner goose.

Confused? Good, limber up those wings, shine those beaks and prepare to get honking.

First though, and before we learn 'the way of the goose', a quick and very true story involving 40,000 superheroes all heading in the same direction.

Fairly recently, I figured that I'd run a marathon, as you do. Have you ever watched someone run a marathon? It's a crazy undertaking that requires months of training and anyone who decides to run one is clearly some kind of machine. Or goose. Or both. Part machine, part goose. Robogoose. I thought that if I was going to commit to this then I might as well run the most famous marathon in the world. A trip to London beckoned.

Even though I ran 26.2 miles and lost all my toenails as a result, I still reckon the London Marathon is to this day one of the most fun, uplifting and inspiring experiences of my entire life. Which is odd, because it's also one of the most painful. Weird, right? What's this got to do with geese? Keep reading.

Sure, a giant Spongebob sprinted past me on the final 100 metres and yes, I was beaten by a tyrannosaurus rex, but I am certain that nothing will ever again compare to the euphoria of finishing the London Marathon. Even without toenails.

It took me 270 minutes to finish. That's a four-and-a-half-hour journey across London, giving me plenty of time to reflect and think about life.

I was pounding the pavement with 40,000 people, each and every one running for a reason. A positive reason. Running with a purpose. Whether that is to win, set a new PB, have fun, raise money for a charity, raise awareness of something meaningful, remember a loved one or support a loved one, everyone was running in the same direction with purpose. (Apart from the guy who ran backwards. Although technically he was still moving in the same direction.)

I didn't win but then again that wasn't my purpose. I was running to raise money for charity in memory of my dad. My only competition that day was myself. But the others played their role in keeping me going.

Super-elite, Olympic-level athletes aside, no one was competing against each other. Quite the opposite. Runners were encouraging each other, helping, supporting, stopping to check on those struggling in the heat and some literally carrying complete strangers over the finish line.

Then there's the crowd. I have no idea how many people line the streets for the London Marathon but it sure felt like millions. Millions of complete strangers, each and every one there for a reason. A positive reason. A purpose. Whether that was to have fun, support a charity, raise awareness of something meaningful, remember a loved one or support a loved one running, everyone was cheering with purpose.

At about 16 miles in, I spotted a spectator holding what looked like a fishing rod. Hanging on the end was a horn, one of those proper old-fashioned horns that you have to properly honk. Attached was a sign that read 'Free Honks to Keep you Going', and boy did I honk that horn. And yes, it kept me going, it made me smile and my energy lifted yet again. I was channelling my inner goose.

This is the very reason geese honk, to encourage others to stick together and keep on going. How cool is that? I basically turned into a goose during my marathon. Well, not really, but it's still cool, right?

Goose Fact Alert

When a goose falls ill, is wounded or shot down, two geese drop out of formation and follow it down to help and protect it. The geese stay with the injured goose until it is able to fly again or until it dies. Then they launch out with another formation or catch up with the flock.

And as if geese weren't already awesome enough, when the lead goose tires, it rotates back into the formation and another goose flies to what's called the point position. They are always looking out for each other, helping, supporting and encouraging.

And this was the big takeaway for me. It seemed that at every moment I began to slow, struggle or hurt – and I assure you there were many. Remember, I started with 10 toenails and ended with none – there was someone or something in place to lift my spirits. It all came from people and their kindness, their humour, their creativity and energy. Just like geese.

It's an incredible sight to see a flock of geese flying overhead in the sky. You'll have noticed they always fly in a V formation. As each goose flaps its wings it creates an 'uplift' for the birds that follow. In other words, by flying in a V formation, the whole flock makes it easier for the geese to stay up in the air. This adds a greater flying range of over 70% than if the birds flew alone.

Goose Science Alert

By taking advantage of the wingtip vortex of the bird in front, each bird can save energy by reducing drag. The energy saved can be as much as 50%.

Just like when I ran the marathon. I was running with others who shared a common direction with a real sense of community. This helped me to keep going, allowing for a tough challenge to feel more bearable. HONK.

Everyone needs free honks to keep them going from time to time. We just need to always ensure that our honking is encouraging. In groups where there is positive encouragement, we achieve more and we'll have a lot more fun in the process.

I can recount tales of fellow runners stopping to help those who were injured or struggling. We all have times in life when we need help, we need someone to come to our rescue.

Be a goose, be a pal, a superhero, a sidekick, a Robogoose, look out for others, be there, create 'uplift', stick together and when you or others need it, HONK as loud as you can. Humans are great, mostly.

Running has changed me forever. I needed to make a positive change. How many times have you heard people banging on about how running helped them not just physically but also mentally? Well, get ready to hear it again.

The way I feel after a run is mind-blowing. I feel a genuine high after a run.

Runner's high is a real thing. Honestly, it exists. But what I've learned is that it only exists after strenuous exercise. In other words you need to push yourself, you need to pretty much knacker yourself. But not overdo it. If you do too much, you'll just feel ill.

The problem now is that if I don't run I begin to feel agitated and my anxiety is more likely to kick in.

To be clear, just like my writing, when it comes to running, I'm not a natural. I'm more Phoebe from *Friends* than Mo Farah. The thought of running 26.2 miles was hilarious, I couldn't even run around the block to begin with. But I did it sensibly, one step at a time, literally. I still hate the actual running part but the way I feel after is magical. I want more of this in my life. So I run more. Simple.

And I appreciate it because one day I won't be able to do it.

In 2018, when my anxiety properly kicked off again, I hadn't been running as often and it definitely had a part to play. Try it, give it three months and you'll be hooked. Let those endorphins do their thing. Trust me, you'll amaze yourself and you'll probably live longer, you big fucking goose!

Honk honk.

5. Read

Books are great. I'm not an avid reader but depending on where I'm at, a book can be my pick-me-up. I love biographies of old rock stars and a good self-help book can definitely help. I also love kids' picture books. Books give us a sense of escapism, occasionally they can give us permission. They can distract us from daily life and keep us in the present.

Here are my top three self-help books:

- **The Art of Being Brilliant** by Andy Cope and Andy Whittaker
- **Tuesdays With Morrie** by Mitch Albom
- **Shine** by Andy Cope and erm, me! Seriously though, it's a really good book!

6. Switch Your Phone Off (Look Up)

I love technology. I'm not a tech geek, I'm not particularly intelligent when it comes to tech and I certainly don't live in a house that's teched up to max with all the latest gadgets and gizmos. But I'm impressed by it.

Just like I'm impressed by engineering. I don't necessarily understand it but I can still be impressed. Planes for example. Show me all the science and breakdown all the workings of a plane and I'll be impressed. But I don't get it. There's no way such a thing can take off and carry hundreds of people *and* their luggage, that's just ridiculous. But it does. Huge ferries don't make sense either. I'm just not clever enough to fully comprehend it. Technology is truly incredible, at times life-enhancing, other times life-changing and, of course, life-saving. If it falls into these categories I'm pretty much all for it.

Kind of.

It can't all be good though, right? Smartphones for example, they can definitely be life-enhancing, the shit you can do now with a phone is unbelievable but again, it can't all be healthy can it?

One of the original commercials for mobile phones sold us the dream of a 'freer life'. Perhaps before SMART technology took over this is exactly what it gave us. But now? A freer life? Really? I have images of Superman wearing his medallion of kryptonite, struggling to move and fighting for energy and air. Drowning almost. Some might consider this a rather dramatic comparison; I'm beginning to think it might be pretty accurate…

Nowadays, telecoms giants have cottoned on to this and offer us a chance to go back. Back to the once mind-blowing days of a mobile phone that allowed us to simply make calls, send texts and play Snake. These once complicated, yet now simple, machines are again on sale. Tempting.

I'm old enough to remember these handsets first time around; strangely I find it once again incredibly appealing. I'm being pulled back in some ways, yet the lure of a new modern handset that allows me to do literally everything is still strong. Perhaps too strong. Maybe I'm hooked, addicted.

We can order our weekly shopping, our takeaway dinners, our taxi, FFS you can basically order your next date. You can record your favourite TV shows, check the score from football fields, check progress from strawberry fields, watch live videos from actual battlefields, turn your lights off, listen to any song you want and you can even post pictures of yourself for absolutely no reason whatsoever other than to be validated by complete strangers who actually don't give a fuck about you.

We can do some cool stuff but there's a side to it all that we know isn't good. Yet many of us choose it. Some of us choose it for our kids, too.

One of the biggest problems we have in our primary schools is bullying on social media apps. Who is letting their child on social media? Who's even buying their child a mobile phone? I always hear the argument, 'but it allows me to keep in touch with my child'.

It's very hard to argue against this. Yes, it does help you to keep in touch. But your 8-year-old needs an iPhone because…?

Ah, that's right, because they fucking don't.

If I could change one thing about the world, I'd switch off social media for kids. We have a generation of parents coming through who don't know any different. If you are a parent and you are allowing your young child on social media then you are fully responsible for that. Not the school, not the teachers. You.

Experts tell us we're in the middle of the biggest social experiment there's ever been. We already know the results and yet we're still going strong.

Just in case you don't know what the results will be, let me tell you: we're fucked.

Absolutely fucked.

We have an entire generation coming through that won't be able to look you in the eye. We have an entire generation who communicate through the medium of thumbs. Imagine how many miles we've scrolled with our thumbs. In a million years our thumbs will be massive. We'll be ruled by thumbs. We'll *be* thumbs.

'Unfortunately, it seems that we, as a society, have entered into a Faustian deal. Yes, we have these amazing handheld marvels of the digital age – tablets and smartphones – miraculous glowing devices that connect people throughout the globe and can literally access the sum of all human knowledge in the palm of our hand. But what is the price of all this future tech? The psyche and soul of an entire generation. The sad truth is that for the oh-so-satisfying ease, comfort and titillation of these jewels of the modern age, we've unwittingly thrown an entire generation under the virtual bus.'

—Nicholas Kardaras, Glow Kids.

Social media. Tell me, what exactly is social about it? Simon Sinek makes a great point about groups of friends all sitting together on a night out staring at their phones. He asks why on earth do they even have their phones, they're with their friends. Again, I can't argue. You might as well have just stayed at home.

I'm certain that we've all had at least one moment (probably many) where we catch ourselves scrolling, just staring at our phones, endlessly scrolling and knowing we should just put it down but even more so *wanting* to put it down…but we don't. We keep scrolling, endlessly scrolling, staring, staring and staring some more. But our thumbs, wow, they're getting strong. Oh and someone 'liked' your heavily filtered duck face. Excellent, well done humans.

Remember when we smiled in photos. That was nice wasn't it?

We spend a lifetime average of 5 years and 3 months on social media. Today alone, more than 3.2 billion images will be shared on social media posts.

Now that I think about it, maybe I would switch it off to everyone…

I became scared of my phone. I've never told anyone this but for almost the entirety of 2018 I had a fear about my phone. I dreaded emails and I'm convinced that social media notifications were making me feel ill at times. I had so much on, actually scrap that, I had *too* much on. Way too much and with 5 different email accounts, 5 different Twitter accounts, 5 different Facebook accounts, 5 different sets of clients and 20 employees all in constant communication, I was drowning.

Notifications are now off. Apps are removed from my phone and trust me, I feel healthier for it.

I still do the social media thing but now I need to log in and I'm moving ever closer to switching off, for good.

'Remember, it's totally fine to put down your phone, look a friend in the eyes and ask if they're ok. Caring is cool.'

—Susan Calman

Turn your phone off for a while. I fucking dare you.

On a side note, Christopher Reeve is the best Superman ever. This has nothing to do with anxiety or this book, but my point still stands: he's the best. And while I'm at it, Superman 2 is the best of the Superman films. Fact.

7. I'm Having the Thought That…

This is one of the best techniques I've ever come across for reducing anxiety and/or removing upsetting thoughts. I learned this from Russ Harris's wonderful book *The Happiness Trap*.

The human mind is such a skilled storyteller. Not only is it skilled in creating the story but it has the unique ability to tell us those stories all the time, forever. It never stops.

The problem for many of us is that the story isn't always the happiest of stories. Some of the daily themes can be rather unpleasant.

Harris teaches us that most psychological approaches regard negative stories as a major problem and make a big fuss about trying to eliminate them. We're told to rewrite the story, think more positively, make ourselves busy and we'll be distracted and on it goes. But the negative story never really goes away.

What we need to do is acknowledge the story but don't give it the time and energy we perhaps would normally unknowingly allocate.

At the height of my anxiety, lying in my bed, eyes wide awake, craving sleep and my chest ready to explode, I simply take the negative thought I'm having, e.g. I'm never going to be able to sleep again, and focus on it for about 10 seconds. Next I take that thought and simply add to it, 'I'm having the thought that…I'm never going to be able to sleep again.' I then run it again and instantly I can feel lifting. Then I do the same again but this time it's slightly longer: 'I notice I'm having the thought that I'm never going to sleep again.' Again, a further lifting. A distance is felt.

It really works for me but it takes practice. Try it now. You'll find in time you are less likely to beat yourself up over negative thoughts and feelings. Remember, thoughts become things. This was a turning point for me. Practice, practice, practice.

8. Hey Google, 'What's wrong with me?'

Dr Google is 100% the wrong doctor to visit when you're feeling anxious or indeed if you have anything at all wrong with you. You can Google 'Why is my ear sore?' and Dr Google will reply with 'brain tumour'. 'Why am I sneezing a lot?' 'Cancer'.

All symptoms tend to lead to some form of cancer; there appears to be no middle ground with Dr Google.

Google is great for real positive information around your personal wellness, just be sure to check credentials and if you're really worried about something it's best to go see a real doctor.

9. Remove the Assholes

We've already looked at not being a dickhead. Now it's time to remove the assholes.

Neighbourhoods, communities, school, work, sport, club, life, the world – we're all a team. The way I see it is we're in this together. And there's no room for assholes.

We all know someone who is a grump, I'm not talking about them. I'm talking about the ones who actively go out of their way to ruin it for everyone else.

Actual assholes.

Negative, arrogant, miserable, bored, egotistical, narcissistic, angry and they love it. They love to share it and drag others down with them, as it makes them feel bloody great. We're all guilty of having a moan from time to time, it can be good to get it off our chests. This is different from being an asshole.

> *'You wouldn't let assholes live in your house – why let them live in your head?'*
>
> *—Hishi Khan*

A friend of mine lives in a lovely wee town on the west coast of Scotland. Her house is in a very quiet street with very little traffic. Outside her house is an enormous van. To be clear, it's huge. About 7 ft tall, 11 ft long, 6 ft wide and to top it off (literally) a selection of ladders. Oh, and it's vulgar. Visually, it's the opposite to aesthetically pleasing. It's aesthetically unpleasing. Disagreeable, pleasureless, unpalatable, displeasing, repulsive, unsavoury, you get the idea. It's an eyesore.

You are perhaps wondering why she has such a van. Well, it's not actually hers and she lives on her own. You might be wondering if it belongs to a neighbour. Nope. The van is not owned by anyone in her street and yet every day it is parked outside her house.

So who owns the van?

The owner of said eyesore lives in another street entirely. When asked if he could move it, he simply said no. When asked if he could perhaps park it outside his own house he simply replied no. When pushed a little more on the subject matter he stated, 'I don't want to have to look at that thing outside my house.'

So just to be clear, this guy knows his van is a big ugly mess, so he has consciously chosen to park it on a different street outside someone else's house, so he doesn't have to see it.

What. An. Asshole.

'Some people will only like you if you fit inside their box. Don't be afraid to shove that box up their ass.'

—Anon

So, I'm going to buy the biggest, shittiest looking van I can, get it insured and park it outside his house.

I'm not really, it would be amazing but hey, I'm not an asshole.

You'll know it's not always easy to deal with assholery and that ignoring/removing them doesn't always work. Over time, an asshole can have a devastating effect on our existence, leaving us feeling traumatised.

Ask yourself if the asshole in your life is temporary or permanent? Assholes are rarely permanent. I don't believe revenge is the right way to go. It feels great in the moment, but the problem is you'll start ruminating and this absolutely doesn't help the way you're feeling. If anything, it makes it worse.

I've thought about doing something to the van, of course I have. But that will come back and haunt me.

Research suggests that karma really does exist, as long as you play the long game.

This isn't new advice for anyone and yet we welcome the Derailers, Negatrons, Mood Hoovers, *Insert own favourite here* into our lives. The difficult truth is sometimes they're family. But if anyone in your life is causing you to feel sad, scared or if they're simply not good for your mental health, then put in the effort to do something about it. Keep a diary of what they say and do. Present it to them in time. But if you need to, remove the ones in your way and actively seek out those who lift you.

10. Say No When You Have To

Saying no to someone is hard. I'm getting better at this. I'm not talking about being busy and adding to your to-do list, although that can cause a lot of stress, I'm talking about the stuff that can make me feel uneasy, anxious and unwell.

Parties, awards nights, certain bookings, weddings, specific family engagements. People can be hugely offended when you say no.

You can offer an explanation if you need to, but when you just know, you know, so say no.

11. Breathe

Seriously, remember to breathe. Not breathing is the number one cause of death. Be sure to keep it going. A good deep breath can fix many a broken thought. Scientists have found that breathing practice is effective in fighting anxiety, depression and stress. Especially proper good belly breathing. The great thing about it is you're doing it right now and it's free and you can do it anywhere.

According to the American Institute of Stress, 'Deep breathing increases the supply of oxygen to your brain and stimulates the parasympathetic nervous system, which promotes a state of calmness.'

Trust me, learning about this stuff was a lifesaver. The biggest surprise for me was how quickly it took me away from the worries in my head and quietened my mind.

12. All We Are Is Dust in the Wind, Dude

In 1989, not too far from Los Angeles, in a small town called San Dimas, Bill S. Preston Esquire and Ted 'Theodore' Logan were dreaming of rock 'n' roll superstardom. What they didn't know then was that they would be responsible for saving the future and become time travelling legends.

No matter where they go, Bill and Ted never stop being 'excellent' to whoever they meet. A most excellent philosophy that I urge the world to get on board with.

Yes, that's right my friends, I am recommending you watch the Bill and Ted movies and always, always, be excellent to each other.

And kind.

And caring.

And giving.

You'll feel better.

The Bill and Ted movies give me hope that there will come a time when everyone is excellent to each other. The world needs it.

Let's finish this chapter with a snippet from the film's theme song, 'In Time':

'In time, we'll be dancing in the streets all night

In time, everything will be all right

It'll take time but we're going far

You and me, yes I know we are.'

Be excellent to each other....and PARTY ON, DUDES!

CHAPTER 8

Let the Wild Rumpus Begin

'A child's world is fresh and new and beautiful, full of wonder and excitement. It is our misfortune that for most of us that clear-eyed vision, that true instinct for what is beautiful and awe-inspiring, is dimmed and even lost before we reach adulthood.'

—Rachel Carson

It's a happy talent to know how to play. Professor Stuart Brown tells us that play is like oxygen. In other words, it's all around us but we just don't notice it.

Until it's gone.

And you know when it's gone. You know when it's gone from your relationship, your friendships and you know when it's gone at work.

When was the last time you had a play on the swings, built a den, made a sandcastle or simply jumped in puddles for no other reason than it's great fun?

Might have been last night, I've no idea but I'm guessing for many out there it's been a while.

Are you too grown up, too sensible, too adult, too cool, too serious? Too *not* playful? Imagine not being playful anymore, it makes me feel sad.

The potential of a puddle becomes overlooked with age…

What would happen if at work, just as everybody was on a massive focus, you were to stand up and at the top of your lungs shout 'FLOOR IS LAVA!'

I'm going to guess almost nothing would happen. A few evil stares perhaps.

Do it in a classroom full of 7-year-olds and you have chaos on your hands. Kids diving onto desks, standing on chairs, sitting with their feet in the air, all the while screaming and laughing.

Or is it chaos? Maybe it's the opposite, maybe it's pure harmony. Just great fun, together in that moment of pure play. All in it together with not a worry in the world, apart from melting in the lava, obviously.

And many of us have forgotten what that's like.

What would happen if you turned up to work on a Monday morning and announced that to kick the week off in style everyone was going to take part in a massive team game of hide-and-seek? Can you imagine the looks? People would think you'd lost it entirely!

Or would they? Would they secretly yearn to join in, to climb into the nearest cupboard, crawl under a desk or rediscover their long-forgotten contortionist skills and climb into a non-human shaped space somewhere utterly un-seekable? But definitely peekable…

Again, do this in a classroom full of kids and BOOM, the week is off to cracking start!

My team and I play hide-and-seek at work. Literally.

I mentioned this recently at a conference and someone in the audience told me I was weird. I asked why she thought this.

'So, you mean to tell me that you and your colleagues play an actual game of hide-and-seek, at work?'

'Yes' I replied.

'Like, *actual* hide-and-seek?'

'Yes' I replied once again.

'Weird.'

'What's weird about it?' I asked.

'A bunch of adults running around playing like kids. At work. That's what's weird.'

'We don't do it regularly, as we're all very rarely in the same place at the same time,' I explained.

'Still weird.'

'How do you start your day at work?' I asked.

'Well, we arrive just before 9 o'clock and we make teas and coffees.'

Woo hoo! Rock. *And.* Roll.

See, the thing is, it's not about the hide-and-seek itself. It's about the vibe it creates. After 20 minutes of playing, can you imagine the buzz in the office? The laughter, the smiles, the energy? That's the feeling we then take into meetings, to the phone, and with us when creating and writing new content.

Having fun and being playful is so much more than having a jolly or mucking about with your pals. It's about happiness, joy, energy, wellness. It's not childish, it's life. It's in our DNA, well, it was anyway…

'I find it amusing that we're all pretending to be normal when we could be insanely interesting instead.'

—Atlas

A couple of years ago I was invited to speak at a TEDx event. This one was particularly special as it was to be held at St Andrews University, one of the most prestigious universities in the world. I was buzzing, couldn't wait to do my thing.

The theme for the day was all around play and rediscovering your inner child. Perfect!

I wanted to try something completely different. I decided my talk would be all about why so many grown-ups don't play anymore, and I wanted to come up with something that would prove it. What could I do in a lecture theatre with 300 grown-ups?

There's no way I could play hide-and-seek; that would be crazy, no one would ever do that. And, plus, it could never work in that kind of space. There's nowhere to hide! And then I began to think, well, that would be perfect because if they really wanted to play then they'd find a way. But in this context it would play into my hands as they *won't* play – because it's crazy – so my point will be proved there and then. As adults we don't play anymore, certainly not the way we used to!

So, hide-and-seek it was.

'You're only given a little spark of madness, you mustn't lose it.'

—Robin Williams

To set the scene quickly, St Andrews University is *well* fancy. I was nervous, partly because it was a TEDx event and partly because I know fine well I don't belong there, our future king and queen went to this university. To be blunt, these aren't my people.

My imposter syndrome was kicking off in all sorts of ways. My self-talk went as follows…

'Shut the fuck up Gav, they've asked you to be here, get in, attempt to play hide-and-seek and get the fuck out.'

That was it, that's all I had for myself in that moment. I honestly don't believe anyone in the entire history of man has had this thought before giving a presentation at St Andrews University.

The room filled quickly. There were 300 people. I was up first. I had 18 minutes.

'Ladies and Gentlemen, please put your hands together and welcome our first speaker, Gavin Oattes.'

I have this habit of forgetting everything I'm going to say as I walk onto the stage and then just as I open my mouth it all comes back to me.

This day was no different. I walked on with nothing, opened my mouth and everything I had planned began to pour out of my mouth. All the while knowing I was building towards my big hide-and-seek moment.

'So, I'm going to shut my eyes and I'm going to count to 10. And you're going to hide.'

There was a ripple of nervousness. In me, yes, but more so the auditorium!

'The rules are you're not allowed to leave the room.'

I'm thinking they'll all just sit there looking at me with a weird expression and this allows me to naturally roll into my main point that as adults we just don't play any more the way we used to, because we fucking grew up.

'If you've never played hide-and-seek before then you've got exactly ten seconds of me counting to Google it and get running.'

I closed my eyes.

'1…'

I hadn't even got to two fucking seconds and all I heard was 300 seats pinging up and 300 people hitting the floor, leaping other seats, screaming, shoving, and laughing their heads off.

Once again my inner voice kicked in…

'Shit Gav, they're fucking doing it. You've got 300 people in a room at the poshest university in the world, it's a TEDx event, it's being filmed *and* they're playing hide-and-seek. Like, actual fucking hide-and-seek.'

I shat it.

What do I do?

Then I had a moment.

A moment of pure fucking magic. And here it is…

Give people the chance to play and they'll take it.

I'll repeat it.

Give people the chance to play and they'll take it.

Think about it. We love to play. You do, I do, we all do. And if you don't love to play then you've never played properly. You've been doing it wrong. Or you've forgotten. I reckon lots of people the world over have forgotten how to play and what it actually feels like to be in that moment.

But how often are you given the chance? We're adults, *we* need *our* hand held. It's all back to front. You were once 4 years old and knew exactly what to do, right? But we've grown up and we've forgotten how to play. We need to be shown. Re-taught. Reminded.

Have you ever watched *Hook* with Robin Williams? It's real. It's fucking real people, look around you.

The whole world has grown up and forgotten what it's all about. Instead we all sit and stare at our phones, as the least playful among us rule the world.

We give every single person the opportunity to grow up and be responsible, prove to the world they can be sensible and make proper grown-up decisions for themselves. We encourage this. We're creating opportunities to be less playful, less fun. That doesn't mean every single person doesn't have fun again, but the reality is that right now the world doesn't feel quite so fun for an awful lot of people. We need to create more opportunities to play. More chances to feel magic.

Soft-play. What do those two words mean to you?

Soft. Play.

What emotions do these two words conjure up for you? I bet you smiled? Even a little? Maybe only on the inside? Imagine how much fun you'd have now at the soft-play. Epic proportions of fun.

But when was the last time someone offered you the chance to go to the soft-play? When was the last time you offered the chance to someone else, who wasn't a child? If you're reading this thinking that soft-play is just for children, then you're wrong, my friend. You can have a happy childhood at any age and soft-plays are now holding adult-only nights. I dare you…

Sandpit.

Fuck I love a sandpit. Maybe it's because I grew up on the west coast of Scotland near the beach, I dunno. But I love them.

I have a sandpit at work.

People think that's weird too. Good. I'd rather be weird than normal, how boring would that be?

If I'm having a crazy busy day or just simply a shit day, I build a sandcastle. The joy is in the building of the castle. The moulding, the shaping, the creating, as grains of sand get everywhere, under your fingernails and in your sandwiches.

And it doesn't matter if someone comes in and destroys it, that's the beauty of sandcastles, you start again. Just like at the beach. It's home time and you know the tide is coming in to sweep it away. Or if you're from where I'm from, a dog's probably gonna shit on it. Wow, maybe there's a crazy world of sandcastle/life metaphors to explore here!

Life is full of disappointments. Even in the most ordinary of moments.

Guess what?

Life is full of fun and wonder. Even in the most ordinary of moments. We're just not being given the chance to experience them. By ourselves. We need to give ourselves these chances as often as we can.

We don't need to save up £15,000 to go to Disneyland for two weeks of fun and games. We need to open our eyes to the wonder of what's around us.

Don't get me wrong, I love Disneyland but I can't afford to live there 365 days a year. I probably would as well.

I also can't afford to spend my (potential) 28,000 days on this planet bored. There's shit to be done.

I *can*, however, afford to smile more. I can afford to go to the beach. I can afford to jump in puddles. I can afford to draw and I can afford to write stories. I can definitely afford to build a den and climb a tree. I can afford to play on the swings and roll down a hill.

And I can definitely afford to go outside and run as fast as I can, for no other reason other than to run as a fast as I fucking can. Remember?

There was a time when all this stuff mattered and filled me up to the brim with joy. Life was like one enormous box of Lego. I could be anything.

I can recall the days when Lego used to claim that a free dinosaur came with every pack, sometimes a free airplane.

Life *is* an enormous box of Lego, we *can* be anything when we're playing. And it comes with a free YOU. Better than any dinosaur or airplane. And you can build your free YOU any way, shape or size you want.

Remember the days when you opened a brand new pack of crayons or colouring pencils? Pure magic, so it was. Hours and hours lost (but not lost) to drawing, scribbling and colouring in. Outside the lines of course.

And where did your artwork end up?

On the fridge.

The fridge was the Holy Grail. You knew that if your masterpiece ended up magnetized to the front of a fridge then you had done something sensational. And of course, it left you bursting with pride.

When was the last time you created something you believed in so much that you put it on the fridge?

And then with time we were encouraged to not rip the paper on the crayons, to not break them and to not scribble outside the lines.

And so it began.

Remember the child you once were? That wee boy or wee girl is still inside you. Still bursting with curiosity, still bursting with excitement.

Still bursting with magic.

STAY WEIRD

What sorts of things did you used to do with your bedsheets?

Tent. Den. Cape. Caterpillar.

My brother used to shove me inside the duvet cover and hang it from the top bunk. I would be hanging in some kind of cocoon as he swung it as hard as he could. It was so much fun, it was just last week.

When was the last time you ran in from work or school, dived onto your bed, rolled yourself up and shouted 'Quick, come and look at me, I'm a sausage roll!'

I dare you to do it today. Dive onto your bed, roll yourself up and shout 'Quick, come and look at me.' Even if you live alone, someone will come running eventually. And when they burst into the room to see what's wrong, you lie there with a very serious face and simply say, 'I'm a sausage roll.'

Look at their face, especially if you've run into the wrong house.

(Evidence to be tweeted to @gavinoattes with the hashtag #ImASausageRoll)

Here's an actual conversation overheard in the school playground recently between a mum and her daughter, who must have been about five.

> **Girl:** But Mummy, I just want to play.
>
> **Mum:** I know but there's just no time to play.
>
> **Girl:** But Mummy, we were seeing who was able to run the most like a bear.
>
> **Mum:** Well, we need to get home because you've got homework to do.
>
> **Girl:** Have you seen how a bear runs?

Mum: What homework do you have?

Girl: Mummy, bears run faster than Usain Bolt and he's the fastest man ever in the world.

Mum: Honey, I'm sure Usain Bolt can run faster than a bear.

Girl: Can I go in the garden and build a den?

Mum: No, it's going to rain in an hour.

OK, so there's a few things I want to pick up about this conversation.

Firstly, there is ALWAYS time to play.

Secondly, there is ALWAYS time to talk about bears. Especially about how fast they are.

Thirdly, bears can absolutely outrun Usain Bolt, FACT!

And lastly, when the fuck do we change from being the person who wants to go out to the garden to build a den and turn into the person who says, 'It's going to rain in an hour'? How depressing?!

'What's the point of even having a garden if no one ever plays in it?'

—Kian Oattes, age 6

Is it as simple as forgetting? Do some of us just forget? Do we just grow up? Are we meant to not play anymore? Is playfulness just childish?

No, playfulness is way more important than we realize.

Game designer Bernard Louis De Koven teaches us that you don't have to play to be playful. You don't need toys or games or costumes or joke books. But you do have to be open and vulnerable, you do have to let go.

And this is something so many of us now find so difficult in adulthood.

He reminds us that playfulness is 'all about being vulnerable, responsive, yielding to the moment. You might not be playing, but you are willing to play, at the drop of a hat, the bounce of a ball, the glance of a toddler, the wag of a tail. You are open to any opportunity. You are loose. Responsive. Present.'

But we're grown-ups. Surely we're all way too busy to be loose, responsive and present?

Well, based entirely on my St Andrews University TEDx experience it would appear not. When given the chance, it turns out many of us will take it. It feels great, it reminds us of simpler times. Fun times.

It's interesting that De Koven talks about presence, about being present. It's such a recurring theme. Yet again, it's all about being in the now. As De Koven reminds us: You have to be present to enjoy the sunrise, to delight in the light of your child's delight, because otherwise you simply aren't there to catch it. It goes by you as if it and you aren't even there.'

'The one thing you have that nobody else has is you. Your voice, your mind, your story, your vision. So write and draw and build and play and dance and live as only you can.'

—Neil Gaiman

This book isn't called *Life Will See You Now* by accident.

Screenwashed

I wonder how much some of us have missed because we were busy or our heads were down…in our screens?

Let's be serious for a moment. You're excellent at play. The best in fact. Why? Because humans are built to play. You're not built to sit staring down at a screen. Scrolling isn't playing.

It's scrolling.

The longer we stare at our screens the less we notice. If we're not careful, by the time we're teenagers, life has become black and white. For too many adults, it's now mostly grey.

Fuck, I'm writing about screens again. But I'm worried. I'm worried about our young people. I'm worried about me.

One of the big telecom giants has been using the following strapline in its recent marketing campaign: **More Data, More Magic**.

No. I think they've got it wrong. I suggest they change it to More Data, My Ass!

They used to tell us 'It's Good to Talk'…

More Data, *Less* Magic. There's nothing magic about more data, more time, more energy, more life spent with our heads down in our screens.

Look around, look what's happening. Kids, adults, parents, whole families lost, lost in a world of more fucking data.

Mums and dads greeting their kids at the school gates with a screen. What about greeting them with a smile?

Families sitting together watching a movie, but Mum's on Instagram, Dad's on Snapchat, big bro is Facebooking, little sis is Pinteresting and we're all having a nosey at our emails.

WHAT ARE WE DOING, PEOPLE?

We're all physically in the room but we're not present!

We're never off, 24 hours a day you have the whole world at your fingertips. Who would dare let their battery run down, who would dare let their phone out of their sight?

As far back as 2008, experts were talking about nomophobia. Now one of the biggest non-drug addictions of the twenty-first century, nomophobia is an abbreviation for 'no-mobile-phone phobia'.

Remember when you could just be? Be in the moment. No need to check your phone every few minutes for notifications. No need to check your 'likes'. Magic.

Actual scientists like Dr David Shaha are telling us that people are spending so much time looking down at smartphones and tablets they are growing bony 'spikes' on the back of their heads. Basically our heads are so fucking heavy that our bodies are having to evolve to accommodate our love of looking down. Children are developing 'text neck' from sitting with their heads dropped forward for too long.

It's time to look up.

I'm introducing POOFO to homes across the world. I've decided it's time for 'Phone's Off Or Fuck Off'. If you're not going to be here with us then go somewhere else and scroll your life away.

And to those who insist on filming *EVERYTHING*. Piss off! Are you documenting your life or living your life?

I dare you to spend more time away from your phone. You'll feel infinitely healthier, calmer, more alive. Our phones even tell us now how long we spend on them. Set yourself the challenge of cutting down. Like cigarettes, sugar or alcohol.

I dare you to switch off, lift your head up and notice.

I dare you to be more present around other people. Around your kids.

I dare you to be more present in your own fucking life.

De Koven says, 'Playfulness means presence, but not just presence. Responsiveness, but not just responsiveness. Presence and responsiveness, lightness and attentiveness, improvization and creativity, a willingness to let go and become part.'

The State of Play

Our ability to let go and play was once ninja level.

My daughter Ellis asked me if she could write a gift list for her 7th birthday. I was intrigued to see what went on it, so I agreed.

Here's the list…

- 400 balloons
- 100 ice lollies
- A stripy door handle

That was it.

That's all she wanted. Balloons, ice lollies and a stripy door handle. What a list!

A STRIPY DOOR HANDLE, PEOPLE!

Why settle for a plain door handle when you can have a patterned one? What a metaphor that is! Let's fill the world with stripy door handles.

When you're a child, every day is an adventure and the world just pops. Trees are greener, puddles puddlier and rainbows seem to have extra colours. Nowadays some kids don't ever see this. The longer we stare at our screens the less we notice. As adults we're noticing less. Some of us perhaps not noticing at all.

We've forgotten that life doesn't need to be plain. It can be even be stripy.

In my daughter's 4-year-old mind she's never very far from a playground. The floor is always lava. Sometimes she plays in the clouds. All steps are rainbow coloured. Every bridge is a shake shake bridge. She never sits still. Homework is fun. Museums come to life. The library is loud and you can borrow more than just books! Waiting never feels like waiting. For Ellis the 'Wet Play' bell doesn't mean we're staying indoors, it means 'Get your wellies on!' It's like every day is national play day.

And most importantly, everyone is invited!

When she was 5 she told me skipping was the 'funnest' way to travel. Try it today, skip everywhere. Skip at work, skip round the supermarket, skip to the loo (my darling).

She's right. It's the funnest!

Now she cartwheels everywhere. It's her current chosen method of transport.

Literally this morning Ellis drew a rainbow, each colour in the order of the song. She then proceeded to cut each line of the rainbow out leaving her with seven colourful arches. Then she walked around handing out rainbow smiles.

This. This is what's missing in the world. Rainbow smiles. And of course those who take the time to hand them out.

Life happens with Ellis and it happens right now. There are no worries about tomorrow and there are never any stresses about yesterday.

To be playful we need to be present, in it, fully. We need a willingness to let go and become part of something.

Ellis turns up at your door and rings the bell.

Three times at least, sometimes a tune.

'Are you coming out to play?'

> Me: How excited are you about going on holiday?
>
> Ellis: I have a summery world in my tummy with 600 shiny stars.

As you read this you'll know that as a child there's nothing actually very hard about being playful. The most difficult part is letting yourself out to play; we may not always spot the opportunity, but the bravest thing is accepting the invitation when it comes our way.

Why do you sometimes stay inside? Why does it sometimes seem so hard to accept the invitation? Especially as an adult.

Far too many young people now worry about looking silly or doing something 'uncool'. We live in a time where we can hide behind screens and present ourselves as anything we want. We are heavily influenced by other people's opinions.

More weight is given to tests and grades than ever. Outside of school, children spend more time than ever in settings where they are directed, protected, catered to, ranked and judged.

Far too many adults feel the same.

When you are playful, you let go of all that. You are not even thinking about being in control or controlling anyone else. You're thinking about fun. And if you see the opportunity, you take it.

A few years ago, along with some colleagues, we attempted to break the world record for the longest bouncy castle relay. Basically, one person needed to be on the bouncy castle at all times and each individual must bounce for a minimum of 15 minutes. There were about seven of us, surely this was beyond doable?

Our thinking was that when we are kids we'll play on a bouncy castle for hours if given the chance. How hard could it be?

Chuck in a bunch of rules and regulations and it changes everything. We were no longer playing, and it was almost impossible. It was no longer fun, it got serious. It didn't feel natural.

We were being tracked and monitored. We failed miserably.

When you are feeling playful, you never think of it as brave to go outside and play or to invite someone to play with you. It feels normal, it can be the most natural thing in the world.

Of course, when you're not feeling playful, it can feel really quite unpleasant, wrong even. You risk being laughed at, made to feel foolish, childish, crazy. And to act playfully, to be playful, given all that, is exactly that: brave.

BUT

When we go for it, shit changes! Being brave, curious, going for it, flying in the face of potential ridicule, opening our eyes to the possible, the wonder of all that is around us, we find fun and play. In fact, we don't *find* it, we *experience* it, we *feel* it, we *become* it, we *are* it, we *are* play, then right there in that moment right with you is a wee thing called happiness.

> *'You're under no obligation to be who people think you are. Change, grow, rearrange yourself. Free and beautiful things always bloom and spark with no holding back.'*
>
> *—Charlotte Eriksson*

It's happening all around us, choose to see it.

And when we play, others join in.

Because it makes us happy.

Be brave. Accept the invitation. Invite others. All others.

All we ever have is now.

Paint stripes on your door handle.

Be more Ellis. Turn up at your mate's house, ring the bell tons of times and ask them if they're coming out to play.

Then on your way home run as fast as a bear and tell your mum all about it!

I dare you.

'I hate all those weathermen, too, who tell you that rain is bad weather. There's no such thing as bad weather, just the wrong clothing, so get yourself a sexy raincoat and live a little.'

—*Billy Connolly*

CHAPTER 9

Once Upon a Time, The End

Factor 50...

It's now over 20 years since Baz Luhrmann gave the world the hugely inspirational 'Everybody's Free'. You may know it better as the 'Wear Sunscreen' song.

Released in 1999, the song – originally an essay by Mary Schmich – gave us various bits of advice on how to live our best life and avoid all the shit that gets in the way of experiencing happiness.

With lyrics inspiring us to enjoy our youth, to imagine, to worry less, to remember compliments and forget insults, 'Everybody's Free' moved a generation to dance, to NOT read beauty magazines and to do something each day that scares us. It encouraged us to travel, be patient and to remember that while friends will come and go, we need to hold on to the precious few.

I wonder if we were to rewrite this song for today how different it would be? If there was ever a time we needed this type of anthem to energize our world, it's now.

There are many lines in this song I'd keep the same and probably a few I'd like to add for modern times. Perhaps right at the start we could add, 'Put your phone down.'

But 20 years on, I can absolutely say with confidence that we *are* reading far too many beauty magazines, we are absolutely *not* dancing enough, and we are certainly not patient enough.

There's more worry in the world than ever and everyone is *not* free, free to love who they want, travel where they want, look how they want, be who they want to be.

But the one line I always remember most and yet never fully appreciated until much later was *'Get to know your parents, you never know when they'll be gone for good.'*

500 Oranges

When I was a child my dad had a great friend, Bill Scott. We didn't see Bill often but when he came to visit, he always brought a gift for my brother and me. Without fail, it was always the same gift, oranges. Not sweets, not chocolate, not toys and certainly never fizzy drinks. Always oranges. And always in a brown paper bag.

Mum was quite strict about healthy eating, something I'll be forever grateful for! Bill knew this and was also – like the rest of us – a little afraid of my mum. Her PE teacher voice was not something to encourage.

We loved the bag of oranges. It always put the biggest of smiles on our faces. So juicy, so colourful, so delicious. And very good for us. I think had it been any other fruit or even sweets for that matter we'd have been disappointed.

Some of our friends didn't get it. 'What's good about a bag of oranges?'

The gift of oranges, why would you ever be disappointed with this? Colourful, fresh, delicious. There is something special and unique about giving oranges and it's stuck with me ever since.

Fast forward a good few years to a conference I was attending where the keynote speaker – a marketing expert – was telling his audience all about the importance of standing out from the crowd and being memorable.

The ironic thing is I can't quite remember all that he said but the one thing I do remember was his piece all about sending mailings in the post. He spoke about 'crushability'. He informed us that when sending things in the post to potential clients as part of your marketing we would need to keep in mind the 'crushability factor'. In other words, the easier the paper is to crush the more likely it is the client will throw it in the bin and never think about you again.

Choose a quality, strong paper with a beautiful shine and guess what? Yup, more noticeable, more memorable. There's the difference, it's keepable. Keepable *is* a word, I checked, isn't it fab?

But even keepable paper can tear, damage or be crushed. It's just *less* crushable, less tearable, less damageable. I've checked, both tearable and damageable are words.

So, along with my team I wanted to deliver a marketing campaign that would be noticed, that people would talk about, remember forever and have no desire to crush.

We wanted to send something in the post that would represent who we are and what we bring within the work that we do. Something different, healthy, bright, colourful, juicy, full of energy and with a big dose of zing. Something that would put the biggest of smiles on people's faces.

It was a no-brainer.

Oranges.

We'll send oranges in the post.

500 of them.

500 big, juicy, bright orange oranges.

'But that's ridiculous, no one sends oranges in the post.'

Exactly.

So, the plan…

Order 500 oranges. We'll package them up beautifully. Not in brown paper bags, too damageable. We'll order beautiful cardboard boxes, fill them with wood wool (posh crepe paper), pop in the orange, add a lovely handwritten label on top and boom, a gift. A gift of health, colour and zest. No covering letter, just a small sticker on the orange with our website on it. Simple.

A few days later we arrived at the post office with 500 lovely gifts ready to send. They looked great.

And off they went first class, for freshness….

Less than 24 hours later 500 oranges landed in the receptions of schools, colleges and businesses all across Scotland.

It was now a case of wait and see what happens. Will our crazy idea capture the hearts and imaginations of the recipients?

The phone began to ring. This was it, the first client to have received an orange. They're calling to tell us how much they love our unique approach, how delicious their fresh juicy orange was and that they wish to book our services....surely?

'HOW DARE YOU DO SOMETHING SO FUCKING STUPID! WHO DO YOU THINK YOU ARE SENDING AN ORANGE IN A BOX TO A SCHOOL, ARE YOU AN IDIOT, DO YOU REALIZE WHAT YOU'VE DONE?'

Now, you can imagine in this moment we were a little taken aback. Not quite what we'd planned or hoped for...

'Sorry, what did you just say?'

'PUT ME ON TO WHOEVER IS IN CHARGE IMMEDIATELY.'

'That's me, Gavin Oattes, Managing Director.'

'ARE YOU SOME KIND OF MORON? YOUR COMPANY BETTER NOT CONTACT US EVER AGAIN.'

I was completely baffled.

'Sorry, who is this?'

'THIS IS THE HEADTEACHER OF *ANGRY* HIGH SCHOOL AND I HAVE ALREADY SPOKEN TO THE POLICE, DON'T BE SURPRISED IF THEY TURN UP AT YOUR DOOR.'

'Why would the police be turning up at my door Mr HolyShitYouAreScaringMe?'

'BECAUSE YOU SENT ME A FUCKING ORANGE, WHO IN THEIR RIGHT MIND WOULD BE SO STUPID?'

I was racking my brains trying to work out if I was missing something. What was so terrible about an orange?

'We did send you an orange but it's part of a marketing campaign. We wanted it to represent who we are as a business. Fresh, different…'

'I HAD TO EVACUATE THE ENTIRE BLOODY SCHOOL.'

'……why?'

'BECAUSE YOU SENT ME A FUCKING ORANGE!'

'I need to ask you to calm down, I'm not quite getting why you're so angry.'

'I THOUGHT IT WAS A BOMB.'

Now, as you can imagine this changed things. This went from being a weird phone call to a seriously weird phone call. A bomb? A fucking bomb?

'Pardon? You thought what?'

Silence

'Why would you think that, sir?…Hello…'

So, by this stage of the conversation I was a little confused and, fair to say, really quite worried.

Almost immediately there was a knock at the door. Yup, it was the police. As I approached the door every single phone in our office was ringing, all our lines were lit up. I could hear the team answering the calls.

'Yes, that's right, it was us who sent the oranges…'

Shit. What was happening? All I could think was, 'What have we done?'

Tentatively, I opened the door and standing before me were two uniformed police officers.

'We're looking for Mr Gavin Oattes.'

Gulp I shat it.

'That's me,' I said. All the while I can still hear the team answering the phones.

'Can we come in please, we'd like to have a chat with you.'

The following is an accurate account of my conversation with the police that very day.

Police Officer 1: 'Have you been sending oranges in the post?'

For a moment I considered lying but I quickly remembered that behind me stood a mountain of large bright orange oranges.

Me: 'Yes.'

Phones are still going crazy

Police Officer 2: 'Why?'

Me: 'We wanted to send something that would put smiles on faces and get people talking. Something that is representative of our business. Different, fresh, full of energy, healthy, etc. etc.'

Both officers glanced at each other as if to approve of our crazy idea.

Police Officer 2: 'Why are you sending the oranges in boxes?'

Me: 'They don't fit in envelopes.'

Both officers nodded in agreement. One nearly smiled.

Police officer 1: 'Why the handwritten labels?'

Me: 'Simply because it looks nice, like a personal gift. A present. They're more likely to open it.'

The phones were still going crazy.

Police Officer 2: 'Why the wood wool?'

Beginning to wonder if this is a set-up, some kind of hidden camera TV show, I replied, 'It looks pretty, a little fancier than crepe paper.'

Again, both officers nodded and appeared to agree with me, it sure was hard to get away from the fact the oranges really were presented in a lovely fashion.

I had a question of my own.

'Have I done something wrong, Officers?'

Police Officer 1: No, actually it's quite a clever idea. Thanks for your time Mr Oattes, we'll be on our way now.

Me: Would you like some oranges to take away with you?

Officers: Aye that'd be great, thanks.

And that was that, they left with a crate of fresh juicy oranges!

I ran – a little flustered – into the office to discover the entire team still answering calls. We had already made more appointments and more sales than *ever* before. Two more schools *had* been evacuated but that aside, we were smashing it. Already our most successful campaign ever.

Next campaign…Watermelons. Even the cops said it was awesome.

So why share this story?

That week we took on 30 brand new clients because we dared to be different. Some people didn't like it and that's absolutely OK with us. We accepted that week that we were never going to be everyone's cup of tea and I'm delighted. It would be boring otherwise.

I've learned over the years that *I'm* also not everyone's cup of tea. I try really hard to be nice to everyone and always be kind and respectful. I have the ability to be a dick sometimes but I'm a hardworking, loving person who gives a shit about people and the world we live in. I don't always get it right, I worry, I fuck up, I'm terrible at housework, I stress, I fear, I anxiety all the way to eleven and sometimes I need to cry about it.

Because I'm human.

Because I'm not perfect.

And neither are you.

Not being perfect is perfection in itself. If you were perfect you'd be bored. You'd also be boring.

Never be afraid to stand out. Be you, be different, be fucking brave. No matter how hard you try in life there will always be them. Those who just don't get it, who don't get you, who just don't see the world the way you do. They just see the mysterious package, they feel threatened. They think it's OK to criticize, bully and in some cases crush you or your ideas.

Send them nothing but love. Nothing but kindness. Nothing but positivity. Nothing but magic.

'Don't ask yourself what the world needs. Ask yourself what makes you come alive, and go do that, because what the world needs is people who have come alive.'

—Howard Thurman

We had three phone calls that day from people who 'flipped their tits'. That's a good Scottish phrase for 'lost the plot'. They went absolutely batshit crazy on the phone because of an orange in the post. Schools receive all sorts of packages and things in the post every day of the year. They jumped to the worst possible conclusion. This says more about them than it does us.

But we had hundreds of other calls that day. Headteachers on the phone stuffing oranges into their faces, thanking us for putting a smile on their face. And, they were damn good oranges!

As the great comedy creation Dave Media once said, 'other people – you = them'.

Our marketing friend from earlier teaches us that humans are fickle. We do judge books by their covers. If something feels weak, we crush it. The reality is this is no different from people.

Bill Scott teaches us that gifts come in all shapes and sizes. His oranges came in a simple paper bag. But what was on the inside was beautiful.

My dad taught me that looks, colour, race, religion, sexuality, gender, ability or size simply doesn't come into it. I should base my judgements purely on whether or not someone is an asshole.

'Watch carefully the magic that occurs when you give a person just enough comfort to be themselves.'

—Atticus

Remember, you don't have to do what everyone else is doing.

You are a beautiful gift. To the world, yes, but to you first.

A beautiful, you-shaped, you-sized, you.

Grampa on the Moon

'What I do is based on powers we all have inside us; the ability to endure; the ability to love, to carry on, to make the best of what we have – and you don't have to be a "Superman" to do it.'

—Christopher Reeve

My dad didn't just introduce me to awesome individuals who gave us the best gifts. He gave me so much more and I've kept this for the last chapter because I've been trying to work out what exactly I'm going to say about him.

Let me tell you about Eric Oattes.

I'll start here…

Before retirement, my dad had two jobs. By day he was a quantity surveyor, which he fucking hated. By night, he was Superman, which he fucking loved.

Now I know what you're thinking. *In chapter 7 you stated that Christopher Reeve was the best Superman ever.* He was, but he wasn't the real Superman. He was the movie Superman. My dad – Eric Anderson Oattes – was the real Superman.

Again, I know what you're thinking. *Superman is a fictional character blah blah blah.*

Wrong.

My dad was actual Superman. Christopher Reeve was chosen to play Dad in the movies because he had black hair and blue eyes. He was the closest they could get without him playing himself, which he couldn't have done because that would let the secret out. Obviously.

In case you're not convinced, my dad wore a Superman suit. I never actually saw it though because by the time we picked him up from work he had dropped it off at the laundry.

The building we picked him up from each evening was cleverly disguised as a small electrical utilities building. To the untrained eye it looked like Dad had just been dropped off there by a colleague who passed that way after work. Not many know this, but it's actually called the 'Fortress of Solitude'.

Dad was careful, he never gave out free rides on his back, there was never any unnecessary flying around the block. There were two very good reasons for this.

1. His suit was in the dry cleaners.
2. The neighbours might recognize him and want a shot.

We even have photographic evidence that my dad could fly.

A wonderful family portrait, Dad sitting front and centre having just caught a baby that had fallen from the sky. A huge swoosh blazing out from behind him as he swooped down from the clouds in the nick of time, all cleverly disguised as a blemish/colour trail in the old-fashioned print. What's especially clever is the fact Dad managed to switch out of his costume and back into regular clothes in time for the photo.

And nowadays he lives on the moon.

Let me explain.

Hey Google, What's Wrong with My Dad?

In October 2010, I received a call from my mum. My dad had been in and out of hospital for tests. He'd been experiencing intense heartburn for some months now. To such an extent that they had decided to run a few tests to rule out anything more serious. He had been told repeatedly things were going to be fine. 'Even Superman gets heartburn.' Probably just some stray kryptonite in the atmosphere…

'Gavin, your Dad has cancer. Pancreatic cancer.'

In that moment everything became urgent and immediate. I can't even begin to imagine how Dad felt sitting on the edge of his hospital bed.

'Six months if he's lucky,' they said.

Fuck this was scary. He's only 63, not even that old I thought. But him and Mum have plans. Bucket-list-sized plans. Selfishly, I began thinking about my own bucket list. Then I kinda went deaf. I could hear Mum talking but I couldn't *really* hear her. What I could hear was my dad. I could hear him in my head telling me of his latest adventures saving the world, defeating evil villains and making sure his costume was dropped off in time for the dry cleaners' closing. Must've been at least 20 years since he'd told me these stories and they all just came flooding back in that moment.

I'm pretty sure my mum mentioned 'the five stages of grief', it's a very Mum thing to say. Ah, the five stages of grief: denial, anger, bargaining, depression and, finally, acceptance. I think I maybe experienced them all in the first five minutes but not necessarily in the correct order. Then came the tears. I was in my car at the time, sitting outside my wife's parents' house waiting to go in for dinner. Fuck I cried. I hadn't cried like this since I was a kid. I remember struggling to get out of the car; each time I went to open the door, the tears began again!

All of a sudden, I could hear again, and Mum was asking if I could pick my dad up from the hospital the following day and take him home. Done.

I didn't sleep a wink that night. Not because my dad had been diagnosed with cancer but because I couldn't think what to say to him.

What do you say to Superman when you realize he's not invincible?

What do you say to your hero when you realize he's not that super?

What will I say to my dad who has just been told he is going to be dead within the next six months, thanks to the most aggressive cancer there is? Five stages of grief? I'm pretty sure that night there were about 25.

The next day I felt heavy. Just heavy. My face, my head, my body, my heart. It was like I'd put on a ton of weight through the night. I was tired from the crying.

I got in the car and headed for the hospital. I sat for a moment on arrival in the hope that I might yet think of something useful to say. Still nothing came.

I found the room Dad was in and stood outside for a while.

Still nothing.

I went in, he had just finished getting dressed. I gave him a hug and asked him if he was ready to go.

I really struggled to look him in the eye.

The drive home was fairly quiet, both of us in deep contemplation. I remember Queen being on the radio. 'Fat Bottomed Girls' to be exact. Of all the Queen songs to come on! Could've been 'Who Wants to Live Forever' or 'Another One Bites the Dust' but no, we had Freddie Mercury singing about how fat bottomed girls make the rocking world go round. Still makes me smile.

It's funny, though, that it should be Freddie Mercury on the radio. Freddie is another hero of mine. My dad and I loved Queen. We used to listen to them when I was a kid, my brother and I often re-enacting Queen's performances. My brother was always on drums (laundry basket), our friend Rory was always on guitar (tennis racket) and I was always Freddie. Always.

When Freddie died in 1991, I fully felt it. Like he was family. He was probably the first person that had ever made me think, 'I want to be on stage.'

I can remember the moment Queen hit the stage at Live Aid like it was yesterday. The man, the voice, the performer, the songs, the way he moved across the stage. Watch it. Look at all those people there, in it. One hundred per cent in the moment. Living every beat with Freddie and of course not one single phone or camera in sight. A kinda magic, I guess.

I loved Freddie. Still do. I remember the first time I saw the video for 'These Are the Days of Our Lives', I couldn't believe what I was seeing. We had heard he was ill, but this was something else. Freddie looked so thin, so ill. I can remember being quite shocked. Moved. Sad. He was just withering away. I had never seen someone looking this way before.

He was a legend.

And legends never die.

But it was now time to witness my biggest hero of all wither away. The legend I loved the most.

I'm not alright with death. I'm really not. I'm not one of the 'I'm comfortable with the fact one day I'm going to die' types. It scares me and I'm keen to put it off for as long as I possibly can. My biggest fear is not seeing my kids grow up.

My dad had set his sights on retirement. He hated his job, moaned about it a lot. But it was all OK because at 65 he was going to get fit and healthy and retirement would give him the opportunity to do all the things he'd ever dreamed of.

'There are only two days with fewer than 24 hours in each lifetime, sitting like bookmarks astride our lives: one is celebrated every year, yet it is the other that makes us see the living as precious.'

—Kathryn Mannix

We arrived home at my parents' house, the very house I grew up in. I told my parents I was going to the loo. Instead I went to my old bedroom. It's a guest room now but it will always be my room. I lay on top of my old bed that I slept in as a child and I just broke down in tears.

My bedroom door opened and in came my dad. I can remember he looked so well in that moment. So calm, so comforting. He lay beside me and put his arm around me and just held me, cuddling me for dear life.

I was 5 years old again.

I was so scared of losing my dad. I couldn't picture in my head who I would be without him.

I've no idea how long we lay there but after what felt like hours he turned and said…

'Now, I don't want any shite music at my funeral.'

My dad went on to fight for 16 months. Described as an anomaly by the doctors, I'd never seen such a transformation in another human being. Mentally he transformed; I'd never known him to be this positive, his entire mindset changed.

But physically he withered away. Again, I'd never seen such a transformation in another human being. He just got smaller and smaller.

My dad died on the 20th of March, 2012. He was 65.

How would I explain things to my 4-year-old son? I didn't have to, he explained it to me.

'Grampa's moved to the moon, Dad. That's where he lives now.' And Grampa on the Moon was created! We've waved to him every day since.

My dad's final words ring true for many of us around the world…

'What the fuck's going on?'

Yes, these were genuinely his final words.

That night I couldn't sleep. I popped on the TV and one of my favourite movies of all time was on. *Field of Dreams*, a film about baseball, that's absolutely *not* about baseball.

'If you build it…he will come.'

'What, what is it?'

'It's my father…'

This is a film about magic, family, forgiveness, redemption, dreams and dads.

I used to rent this movie from the local video shop when I was in my early teens. The first time I saw it I loved it but what I didn't expect was the ending. It broke me there and then.

'You want to have a catch?'

If you've never seen it, *Field of Dreams* has the greatest father–son moment in cinematic history. I urge all the sons out there and all the fathers to make a man date and get this film watched together. I warn you now though, you might want to practise your best 'I've got something in my eye' routine!

To be able to play catch with my dad one more time…

Just at this moment my own son, then aged 4, appeared beside me, as if by magic.

'What's this, Dad?'

Quickly wiping all the snot and tears from my face, I replied,

'It's a movie all about a young man who hears voices in his head and it leads him to build a baseball diamond in his field and then lots of ghost baseball players appear and one of them is his dad and they get to play catch one last time…'

I felt like I was having my own Hollywood moment, I looked at my son, hugged him and asked:

'Do you want to play catch? Right now, even though it's the middle of the night?'

His wee face lit up, he stood up and said,

'Nah, I just needed a jobby.'

I haven't been able to watch it since.

I Hate Goodbyes

My dad loved a cigar. He didn't smoke them regularly, but he had boxes of them in hiding. Good ones too, not just the cheap ones.

The night before his funeral my mum suggested it would be a nice idea to hand out all my dad's cigars to those in attendance the following day. We all agreed this was a lovely thing to do in Dad's memory.

Mum being Mum then suggested we wrap each one individually with a lovely red bow. She had stacks of ribbon lying around that could be cut to size and tied beautifully, each cigar presented as a beautiful gift.

With cigars, scissors and ribbon all laid out on the table, five of us sat around the table and prepared our production line.

Just as we all reached out to begin, every light in the room flickered and buzzed. It had never happened before and with eyes wide open we all just sat and looked at each other. In any other circumstances we probably wouldn't have given it a second thought. We just sat in silence.

We reached out again for the ribbon and once again all the lights flickered and buzzed.

Surely not…

Could it be that the thought of all his favourite cigars being given away was enough to bring him back from the dead to send a powerful message? My dad loved to share his cigars, so I like to think it was the pretty red bows he was pissed off about.

We ditched the red bows and the lights never flickered again!

When something is what it is, then perhaps we don't need to wrap it up and present it as something it's not?

Like we do on social media using filters, filtering our faces until we no longer resemble our true self.

Freddie Mercury was right when he sang…

'Open your eyes, look up to the skies and see.'

The world is beautiful and so many of us don't see it. We're too busy. We're too busy trying to be something we're not. Too busy trying to be a version of ourselves that's not making us happy.

There's way too much shit in this world that we're allowing to get in the way of what truly matters.

Life just gets faster and faster. Before you know it, you and everyone around you will be dead.

'I'm sad, but at the same time I'm really happy that something made me feel that sad. It's like, it makes me feel alive, you know? It makes me feel human. The only way I could feel this sad now is if I felt something really good before, so I have to take the bad with the good. So I guess what I'm feeling is like, the beautiful sadness.'

—*Butters,* South Park

Far too many of us are spending our time agonizing over all the shit that doesn't matter.

In Chapter 1, I called it. Born, live, die. Two out of three guaranteed. A life and death sandwich. But what are you having? A shit sandwich or a gourmet deli delight?

From a young age we are taught that every great story has a beginning, a middle and an end. We need middles.

It's where the bulk of the story rests. It holds the reader's attention, but most importantly it is where we reach the climax or turning point of the story. The middle is just as important as the beginning and the end. If the middle is good, the reader will remain invested.

My friend is a novelist and she told me all about the 'sagging middle', an issue that novelists work hard to avoid as they construct their story. Sounds like something I face when I don't exercise enough.

Remember, the middle is the hard part. It's the bit where you need to actually do the work. To combat a 'sagging middle' requires more work than normal but it's entirely worth the effort. And then when we get to the end of our story, there's no looking back with regret.

There's a ton of research out there highlighting the regrets that adults have towards the end of their life. No one ever regrets spending too little time online, no one ever wishes they'd had more Wi-Fi, everyone wishes they'd worried less and they all speak highly of family, music and ice-cream.

Same goes for children. Dr Alastair McAlpine spends every day caring for children with life-threatening and life-limiting illnesses. He recently asked his young terminally ill patients what they enjoyed most in life and then shared it on Twitter.

> First: NONE said they wished they'd watched more TV. NONE said they should've spent more time on Facebook. NONE said they enjoyed fighting with others and NONE enjoyed hospital.
>
> MANY mentioned their pets. MANY mentioned their parents, often expressing worry or concern: 'Hope mum will be ok. She seems sad.' 'Dad mustn't worry. He'll see me again soon.'

> ALL of them loved ice-cream.
>
> ALL of them loved books or being told stories, especially by their parents.
>
> MANY wished they had spent less time worrying about what others thought of them, and valued people who just treated them normally. 'My real friends didn't care when my hair fell out.'
>
> MANY of them loved swimming, and the beach.
>
> Almost ALL of them valued kindness above most other virtues: 'Jonny gave me half his sandwich when I didn't eat mine. That was nice.'
>
> Almost ALL of them loved people who made them laugh.
>
> Kids loved their toys.
>
> Finally, they ALL valued their time with their family. NOTHING was more important. ”

I simply can't disagree with any of this.

Kids. Just. Know.

So basically, in summary…

Offline. Kindness. Fun. Ice-cream. Family.

My dad may have taught me to worry more (d'oh!) but he also taught me to turn the TV off and get outside. He taught me to love stories, to swim, to be kind, to appreciate laughter, to love my pets and my god did he teach me to love my family. And life.

He taught me the importance of happiness.

He taught me to replace what-ifs and should-haves with fuck-yeahs and no-regrets. And slowly I'm getting better at this. But it takes practice.

I learned quickly that my dad's role in life had been so much more to me than joke teller and drinks pourer! I got to know him really fucking well when he was alive but in some ways I got to know him better once he was gone.

One year later – to the very day my Dad died – the 20th of March was declared 'International Day of Happiness' by the UN General Assembly.

Jayme Illien chose 20th March for its significance as the March equinox, a universal phenomenon felt simultaneously by all of humankind, and which occurs the moment when the plane of earth's equator passes through the centre of the sun's disk.

I don't even know what this means but it sounds so fucking cool.

UN Secretary Ban Ki-moon said, 'Happiness for the entire human family is one of the main goals of the United Nations,' and called upon all human beings to 'dedicate our efforts to filling our world with happiness.'

So let's do just that. Let's dedicate our efforts to filling our world with happiness.

Not just on 20th March.

But every day.

Even though we can't be happy all the time, the idea of happiness being a 'universal phenomenon felt simultaneously by all of humankind' is for me, something worth fighting for.

And you're all invited.

So, step outside right now, take a big deep breath in, and as you breathe out remember who the fuck you are.

In the words of Bomi Bulsara, I wish you nothing but 'Good thoughts, good words, good deeds'.

I hope you've got at least one ice lolly built into your day today.

Merry everything and happy always.

Carpe that fucking Diem…

Acknowledgements

I fell in love with my wife Ali the day I met her; I was 19 years old. I told her I was writing stand-up comedy and that me and my best mate Rolls were going to be huge. She didn't even flinch. We didn't make it. She still didn't flinch. She's the most supportive, honest, hardworking person I've ever known. And 100% out of my league.

To my parents, thank you for giving me the belief to follow my heart always. Obviously, I was the perfect child and made your life incredibly easy...

My truly wonderful children, Kian and Ellis. You are the best thing that has ever come out of life. You just make every day worth it; I cannot express how much I love you both.

And finally, to Frank Epperson for inventing the ice lolly. Dude, you nailed it.

About the Author

Gavin Oattes is a once-in-a-lifetime type of human. Think Optimus Prime meets Freddie Mercury meets Mary Poppins. Someone who just simply wants to inspire the world, help others to help themselves and always, *always* put on the best show possible. He also happens to be an award-winning entrepreneur, award-winning comedian and a bestselling author. Book him as your keynote speaker and learn just why some of the biggest companies in the world turn to Gav to inspire their people. He lives in Edinburgh, Scotland with his wife, two children and his cat, David Bowie.

Keep Up with Gav

Twitter: @gavinoattes
Facebook: @gavinoattes
Instagram: @gavoattes
Website: gavinoattes.com

Index

ALSO BY **GAVIN OATTES:**

SHINE: Rediscovering Your Energy, Happiness and Purpose

Andy Cope & Gavin Oattes
9780857087652 • £10.99

Find out just how easy it is to boost your energy and increase your motivation. Discover how to break free from 'ordinary' and embrace a life of 'extraordinary.' Figure out how to channel your inner Mary Poppins or Peter Pan. The self-help book that people read again and again.

ZEST: How to Squeeze the Max out of Life

Andy Cope, Gavin Oattes & Will Hussey
9780857088000 • £10.99

When life gives you lemons, it also gives you ZEST. *Zest* is a wake-up call for you to explore the formative moments that define your life. It challenges you to believe that your best days are still ahead, to search your soul, to shake things up and bask in the warmth of glorious individuality.

DIARY OF A BRILLIANT KID: Top Secret Guide to Awesomeness

Andy Cope, Gavin Oattes & Will Hussey
9780857087867 • £10.99

The "tweenager's" atlas for navigating life.

"Diary of a Brilliant Kid was very, very, very good. I've got lots of tips and it was very funny. I like how it gets more factual as the story goes along and I wish there was a sequel"

Isobel, Age 10 ★★★★★

AVAILABLE FROM YOUR FAVOURITE BOOKSHOP OR ONLINE

CAPSTONE
A Wiley Brand